THE SCROLL

&

THE SEAL

NIGERIA: A DESECRATED NATION WITH A PROPHETIC DESTINY

~Publication Date: November 29, 2018~

Ebenezer & Abigail Gabriels

EGƎ

Ebenezer Gabriels Ministries

www.ebenezergabriels.org

hello@ebenezergabriels.org

ISBN:9781950579143

~Publication Date: November 29, 2018~

the United States Copyright law.

DEDICATION

Adonai Adonai
Release your cloud of presence, Over Nigeria
Adonai Adonai
Release your cloud of glory, Over Nigeria

As we wait on you
Let your glory fill Nigeria
Let your presence fill Nigeria

Adonai Adonai
Release your cloud of presence, Over Nigeria
Adonai Adonai
Release your cloud of glory, Over Nigeria

This song was given to us in worship. The song tells the story of God's companionship with Israel, His inheritance. When Israel came out of oppression from Egypt, the Scripture notes in Exodus 13:21 that the LORD went ahead of them in a pillar of cloud during the day and at night in a pillar of fire to give them light. This song is our prayer for Nigeria, that the cloud of His presence and glory will be released over Nigeria; as Nigeria returns to the Lord.

CONTENTS

INTRODUCTION

The Scroll & The Seal uses a series of personal prophecies given to us during intense worship encounters and the Nigerian Pentecostal Church history to shine light on some of Nigeria's perplexing enigmas and how God is set to turn the Church back to Him with the outcome of 2019's presidential election. In *The Scroll & The Seal,* we discuss prophecies given to us from 2016 through 2018, their meanings; manifestations and how they tie back into Nigeria's Pentecostal history and the prophetic future of Nigeria. *The Scroll & The Seal* is centered on critical examinations of prophecies we received from the Lord and uses these divine insights to increase understanding of the current state of the Nigerian Pentecostal Church circles and the nation Nigeria.

This book originally evolved in 2016 as notes captured during encounters with the Holy Spirit and shared with our network of praying worshippers for the purpose of intercession. It has subsequently become a compilation of prophecies, research and underlying issues challenging nations, government, politics, communities and especially the Church. In this book, the Holy Spirit opens up mysteries behind the many problems of Nigeria and a way out.

As God's prophetic mouthpiece, we communicate the heart of God as He instructs us to. *The Scroll & The Seal* is for all and those whose hearts are given to or seek to be given to intercession for Nigeria. Here is the threefold message of *The Scroll & The Seal*: Judgment is coming to Nigeria because of the iniquities of the Church; Salvation is assured if the Church leads the nation back to Him; Revival is coming to Nigeria which will catapult Africa to the world stage in the coming years in the areas of technological breakthrough.

Although we write on a range of topics in this book, we must admit that we are not historians, theologians, or politicians. Our writings are primarily motivated by the Holy Spirit to communicate God's heart to the Church. In the days of Moses and the times of the Prophets Isaiah, Jeremiah, Ezekiel and Daniel, we read stories of how the Lord spoke through them. God still speaks, beyond a shadow of doubt. He has never changed, and He will never change. We are Nazarene worshippers of YHWH, a husband and wife team with hunger for the move of God, and in the service of Jesus; on the mission field and in the marketplace. We are passionate readers of the Bible, privileged to have the Holy Spirit as our teacher. We take time to consume and meditate on a good dose of the Scriptures daily. From Church planting, to leading street worship, praying for the sick and winning souls for Jesus, we avail ourselves to the service of the Kingdom of God. We are praying that others will discover the hidden treasures of God that are hidden in worship.

Nigeria has a prophetic mandate to fulfill in the global Church. A strong reason for Satan's rage against Nigeria. Nigeria's current deteriorative state has little to do with the government, but a lot to do with the Church. The

Church has ventured into all sorts of iniquities. In a vision, the Lord paints a picture of a Church who is supposed to set the direction for the nation but thrives in iniquity, sets the nation decades backwards and is about to bring wrath upon the nation. How has a prophetic country degenerated into a funeral nation with dead bodies littering the streets? The bloodshed by government leaders, occult people camouflaging behind the pulpit, the kidnapping rings, prostitution trade, moral corruption that permeates our communities; God sees it all - hoping His people who are called by His name would humbly repent from their wicked ways and turn back to Him.

The time is now to turn from our wicked ways. The time is ripe to stop pointing fingers to others, but to become Nigeria's intercessors and be the ambassador of Jesus by living a life that reflects Jesus, His grace, His salvation and His power and love. We must never forget that our righteousness has the power potent enough to exalt Nigeria.

1

THE MYSTERY OF THE SCROLL & THE SEAL

Scrolls contain cryptic and important information in the Scripture. In a few Scripture instances, scrolls were symbolic with information storage especially in the prophetic ministry of prophets like Jeremiah and Ezekiel. Some scrolls contained information and others were tools for information capture. Before the 66 books of the Bible became one combined book, the earliest Bible texts were written on scrolls.

It is the nature of God to keep secrets. When the Lord is about to do a thing, He opens up those secrets to people who are intimate with Him. Why? To declare His plans and give warnings of things to come. Justice is the foundation of His throne, yet and He is full of compassion. That's why He sends out His word to give hope, warn of impending judgment and call people back to righteousness. God gives people and nations time to repent. He extends grace to them, awaiting change of hearts. This is one of such instances that the Lord has given His word concerning His plans to call Nigeria back to righteousness through punishment, if the Church fails to repent. The upcoming chapters are accounts of revelations the Lord has given to us to share with Nigeria.

THE SCROLL OF JESUS

Wisdom abounds in Heaven. Mankind needs wisdom to sail through life successfully. The questions we must ask are; how can wisdom be accessed? How much of God's wisdom is available in our times of abundance of demonic wisdom? At what interval is wisdom released to the nations? At what frequency is wisdom released to us? Where is the dwelling place of wisdom?

Like radio frequencies, wisdom is broadcasted from God's throne in Heaven to the earth at all times, but only a few catch the signal. These are the ones covenanted with Jesus by the sacrifice of worshipful living and consecration.

If anyone dwells outside the realm of God's access, the way through the curtain into His presence is becoming more like Jesus. Such is the grace we now enjoy, only if we understand that grace is extended to us so that our capacity is increased to conform to the image of Jesus, and not a license to squander God's mercy or make a ridicule of the blood of the Lamb that was poured out for our salvation.

The mystery of scroll is endless. The Scripture gives us some insights. Ezekiel was given a scroll to eat, signifying the words He received from the Lord. Jeremiah's prophecies were written in a scroll and read in the house of the Lord to the people in Jerusalem. Zechariah saw a scroll in flight which represents a curse flying into the house of disobedient people. There was a unique scroll, different than the one Jeremiah had, than the one Ezekiel ate, and not similar to the one Zechariah saw in flight. In the fifth Chapter of the book of Revelation, a new scroll surface, "the Special Scroll of Jesus Christ". In the revelation given to John, Jesus was the only one found qualified by all standards to open the seals of the scroll.

The most common feature of a scroll is that it is for a defined audience, whether a nation or an individual. Unlike the other scrolls described in the Scripture, the Jesus' scroll was reserved inside the Throne Room of Heaven. The scroll was of great significance that it was not sent through multitude of angels of God; John had to be brought to the location of the scroll. A scroll of such importance could have been locked up in a vault, but it was not. It was on the right hand of HIM who sat on the throne (*Revelation 5:1*). Only Jesus' signature could take the scroll out of the hands of the

Father, and the key to break the seal and open the scroll dwells in the blood of the Lamb. Some might wonder, why did it have to be Jesus? The revelations from the heart of God is revealed to us through the Jesus Christ, based on his qualifications of purity, righteousness and blood sacrifice. He is the only one worthy to access the document bearing the secrets of the world, and things to happen on earth.

This point to only one conclusion, Jesus is the only way to wisdom.

THE SCROLL & SEALS OF THE NATIONS

When you request your transcript to be sent out from your high school to a university, the transcript is placed in an envelope for protection and privacy. That's a first level seal. Then a second seal comes on; stamp by the school's office of academic records is used to seal the envelope. That tells the university that the document truly originated from your high school. If the seal is broken, the receiver may reject the transcript. The same logic applies to food items or body cleansing substances. Manufacturers always warn consumers not to use products with broken seals because the consumer is expected to be the only one with access to the products in the container, not the retail. A broken seal on a product could mean the content of the container is compromise.

Similarly, every nation has its unique scroll. It contains secrets to the nation's successes, failures, and God's plan for the nation. When the Lord desires, He takes a portion of the scroll and reveals it to His servants, not for the fun of it but to set a change in motion. Ezekiel was fed a scroll and sent to the house of Israel. Jeremiah's scroll was released to him for the warning of the house of Judah.

The seal is the locking up of the scroll for each of those nations. The seal is the key to the scroll. There are scrolls but they are hidden. When the seal is broken, access to the scroll is given. When you hear a seal, think of an envelope on a document. Think of a seal as the covering of a package holding an important document. Seals are attached to documents for authentication or access.

THE SCROLL EXPLAINED

In most of the scrolls in the Bible, the prophets were given information through visual cues they could relate with. God speaks to us in plain language. In words we can understand, through symbols we can identify. The scroll is the wisdom of God. It is only released to His children through the spirit of prophecy. And that is the reason why the angel told John, *"the testimony of Jesus, is the spirit of prophecy"* in Revelation 10:19 because true prophecies reveals the glory of the Lord, bear witness to the power of the Lord Jesus and releases Heaven's wisdom to the earth.

THE BLAST OF WISDOM ON THE STREETS

While growing up in Nigeria, noise pollution was

rampart; starting from the cock crows in the early hours of the morning to the melodious advertising slogans of the food vendors on the streets. There were also the Evangelists on the bus, who would share the gospel tirelessly as people travel from one location to the other. There were also the ones who sold Christian albums and booklets at the bus stops. They will always have your attention. That is the way of wisdom. Wisdom is as loud as those street vendors. No matter how loud wisdom sounds, only a few yield to the call of wisdom. "Wisdom shouts in the streets. She cries out in the public square". We see a similar occurrence in Proverbs 1:20 when wisdom is blaring her instructions and the people are carried away with the sensations of demons that hinders the entrance of the Word. The spirit of wisdom says the words of Proverbs 1: 20-23 to the Church in Nigeria:

> "Out in the open wisdom calls aloud, she raises her voice in the public square; on top of the wall[she cries out, at the city gate she makes her speech: "How long will you who are simple love your simple ways? How long will mockers delight in mockery and fools hate knowledge? Repent at my rebuke! Then I will pour out my thoughts to you, I will make known to you my teachings.

The picture of wisdom painted above tells us that though the Lord showers us with abundance of wisdom, it not widely accepted. Though the truth is right is our faces, only a few will open up and receive the truth.

THE SCROLL OF NIGERIA : TRADE BY BARTER

Nigeria, a country with millions of Churchgoers and thousands of growing Churches, has a prophetic role to play in the world. The enemy knows this and has raged rigorously against the destiny of Nigeria. The scroll of Nigeria contains critical piece of Nigeria to solve not only Nigeria's complex puzzle, but also a key to breakthroughs for other African nations, world economies and the global body of Christ. At this time, the nation is nowhere close to the picture of its prophetic destiny.

Questions have been asked as to why Nigeria is walking faraway from its destiny. Some questions include:

- Why are the numerous Churches not effectively interceding for a prophetic nation under captivity?
- Does majority of the Church leaders speak to God about the destiny of Nigeria?
- Why is there so much moral decline in the Church? Where has decency fled?
- Why do we now have female ministers who dress half-naked? Why has the Spirit of wisdom departed from majority of the Church?
- If majority of the Church does not hear from God any longer who is she taking instructions from?
- Why has the new generation Church become a place of feasting and not a house of prayer and worship?

Only God has these answers. There is no other establishment graced with the sole access to some of these answers than the

Church. Some of these answers are answered in upcoming chapters.

God has given the Church in every nation the keys to the seals securing hidden treasures contained in national scrolls. The mysteries of Nigeria's failures and successes have been given to the Church in Nigeria. Because the Church has perverted the gospel of Jesus and departed from the way, the access to the national scroll has been withdrawn. The Church will never be able to make sense of the way forward for Nigeria until the Church repents and fully to the Lordship of Jesus.

The Church in Nigeria has underestimated its role in the prophetic destiny of the global Church of Jesus Christ. Satan has bewitched the Church, and the Church is taking the bait. We are assured that the gates of hell will never prevail against the Church. The enemy continues to wreck more havoc through the Church in order to mar the prophetic destiny of Nigeria. If the Church continues to resist the devil without being in submission to the Lord, the voice of the Church will have no positive influence on the nation.

2

CALLED TO WORSHIP

Like my old self, many were born and raised in the Church, served in the Church and even directed the worship team seamlessly. Many who were part of the "worship experience" would come to say afterwards, "*Ebenezer, the worship was so anointed*". As good as that sounds, many of those statements were mere flattery with no element of truth in it. There is no anointing without consecration, there is no anointing without brokenness, and there is no anointing in sin. There is no anointing in pride; neither does the anointing function effectively in the flesh. With the anointing, you wear the name of the Most High as a blanket and as your inward apparel; you also bear the seal of holiness to access God's presence - a place where no unclean thing can reach. The anointing is a pricey privilege. Where you see the anointing, heavens open, and yokes are crushed.

ANOINTED VS TALENTED

The devil is a subject matter expert at deception. He understands the nature of the anointing and has cloned his version, wrapped in deception, and presented it back to the unsuspecting as the real deal. The best cartoons and animations are not necessarily done by those who have the best drawing skills but done by those who have a better understanding of word arrangement and the manipulation of emotions. This is how the enemy has messed up people's mind about the subject of worship.

Everyone who has been given access into the realm of the Holy Spirit knows that talent goes nowhere before the Lord. The proof of anointing is that the anointing shatters yokes and gets Heaven's backing. The anointing is not cheap. It requires sacrificial living, deeper consecration, maturing in the Word of God and continual communion with the Holy Spirit. Talent without the anointing is like an off-the-shelf solution. It is fancy and can be easily decorated like an icing on the cake.

An individual may be very skillful in playing musical instruments, but not anointed to worship. Anointed musicians would humbly submit themselves only as vessels to bring the people into God's presence. Like many, I was prideful of my talents and I would think because I was born and grew up in the Church, I knew God. The weight of the anointing can only be carried safely by broken vessels who are totally dead to the flesh. This was the way of the prodigal son, who squandered grace until the hands of the Lord snatched me from a nearly destructing experience. The multitude of His many kindnesses that brought me to repentance.

NAZARENE WORSHIPPERS

Looking back at the years of growing up in church, leading worship without being in Jesus. I had questions. How did I not know the Lord all these years and I thought I did? How did I fall away from the apostolic foundation? In the place of asking these questions, my wife and I met the Lord in numerous rare encounters. For the very first time, I encountered the Lord tangibly, and we began a new walk with the Lord, desiring the everlasting pleasures at His right hand.

CALLED TO WORSHIP & INTERCEDE

One of the first places every Nazarene worshipper finds themselves is in the place of intercession. Intercession is fueled by a rare type of love, flowing from the heart of the Father, through the Holy Spirit to the worshipper. Same kind of love at work in the life of the Lamb of God. An unfathomable kind of love. Intercession is loving people you may never know. Intercession is loving people you may never see. Intercession is connecting to the love in the heart of the Father. Intercession is all about pure unadulterated love. Intercession is travailing in prayers for others, and sometimes, intercession is a rare type of mercy received by people.

We received mandates from the Lord to intercede for nations, communities, leaders, friends, and also people whose name we never heard of. We obeyed. Our prophetic mandate is summarized thus: revive worship altars, uproot wickedness from foundations and intercede for the nations. Immediately through our actions, we said to the Lord, "Father, sign us up instantly for whatever you are doing". Surprisingly, we got to work immediately. There were numerous assignments awaiting us already. The most surprising moments were days sometimes weeks after our interceding news alerts would pop on our phones or someone from our prayer meetings would send a link to the news. One of the saddest news was when we saw a school bus with kids involved in a bus crash. We went into prayers immediately. A few weeks after, the news came, none of the kids were killed or injured, but the driver died. We did not pray for the driver. We wished we did and learnt from this experience

PENTECOSTAL ENCOUNTERS

At the former Elementary School where our home Church- LightHill gathered to worship, there was a man who was on the security team. He joined the school the second week we began meeting at that location. He opened the door to the building for us each week. After a few weeks, the Lord said he was promoting the man for his faithfulness. He later came to share with us that he had become the Security Manager. We were happy for him.

Our worship continued weekly. During one of our Bible Study Classes, the whole Church studied the book of Revelation. It was critical. It was important for us to study what it is to come at the end. After the book of revelation, we proceeded into the book of Acts. We studied the book in detail, and very slowly, so that we would not miss a thing. The Act studies went powerfully that people who didn't speak in tongues began to speak in tongues and we encountered miracles. The last study from the book of Acts was on the Sunday of May 2017; the day of Pentecost. Such a powerful alignment! Then the Lord spoke His word over the gentleman who managed the security team, "I am promoting you and taking you into a place of blessing". The Lord also said, "This community will be blessed, and children from this school will be known for excellence everywhere they go, and the glory of the Lord shall follow them". The worship service was over and we all departed the Church.

The next Tuesday, we got the call from the School administrator that the part of the school where we met would be going under renovation for 3 months. That means we would have no place to gather for worship. The school gave us one week to move. Three days after, we got another phone call from an agent who told us a new location was available and the key was ready for pick up. We moved the same week - the week of Pentecost. With how this played out, we all felt the Elementary School where we gathered was like our Jerusalem where the Lord wanted us to stay to load up on the word of God and be fully immersed in the Holy Spirit before we launched out. And when the day of Pentecost on the Jewish calendar came, it happened again as it was in the times of the Apostles.

Acts 1:4

> On one occasion, while he was eating with them, he gave them this command: "Do not leave Jerusalem, but wait for the gift my Father promised, which you have heard me speak about.

With prophecies, when the time of manifestation comes, only those in the spirit would catch it. We missed what the Lord was doing up until our last day at the Elementary School. It was like a farewell prophecy the Lord gave to the Security, the School and the community. It was the last time the Church was meeting at that location. The body of Christ didn't know, but of course Jesus knew what He had in stock for His body and when He was going to launch his body forth after the day of Pentecost had arrived.

The power of the Holy Ghost is alive and active. Although many have tried to misrepresent the Holy Spirit due to their non-existing relationship with Him. The move of the Holy Spirit is the picture painted in Acts 1:8 followed by a proof as shown in Acts 2 and beyond. Wherever the Holy Spirit shows up, He comes to power up a situation to fuel it for efficiency. The Holy Spirit brings power into powerless situations.

MONTGOMERY VILLAGE REVIVAL

As we moved into the new place of worship, the Lord said, "This community is about to be turned upside down. Things are turning around spiritually in this community already. The hand of the Lord is upon Montgomery Village. There's an exchange of power in the spirit realm and the power of YHWH is manifested and about to be displayed".

Last September, we gathered to study the final chapter of the book of Daniel, a revival broke out. A 2-hour Bible Study lasted 8 hours. And it continued that way for 7 days. There was no schedule; everyone came hungry for the knowledge of God. Each day, we worshipped at length and studied the Scriptures and discussed the power of the Holy Spirit. That's very strange in a country like America where people stick to schedule. Our testimony was Psalm 27:4 in action, "One *thing* I have desired of the Lord, That will I seek: That I may dwell in the house of the Lord All the days of my life, To behold the beauty of the Lord, And to inquire in His temple". We didn't desire to leave God's presence for any reason. People went home to shower to get to work the next day. By 7pm the next day we all returned to the Church, no plans, no schedules, just to worship and discover God. We met again Thursday, Friday, and Saturday. And I said, what's happening? God led us to Psalm 110:3 "Your people shall be willing in the days of your power". We looked at our calendars and found out it was the days leading to one of the appointed times of the Lord, the feast of the Trumpets. We were so humbled that the word of God was fulfilled amongst us, "These are My appointed festivals, the appointed festivals of the Lord, which you are to proclaim as sacred assemblies" - Leviticus 23:2. On Sunday we met twice. Morning worship and the evening revival crew met and again we met on Monday, September 10 and then on Tuesday September 11, 2018. The outpouring of the Holy Spirit is never planned but must be prepared for. As a river, it can never be contained in the confines of programmed events. For 7 days, it rained, and people from different works of life gathered and faithfully for an unplanned move of God, breaking the hedge of their regular sleep hours.

The Feast of the Trumpet signifies the coming day of the Lord, the prophetic day that the trumpet is blasted as a warning of the big day to come. As a Church, we found that the Lord arranged the days leading to the Feast of Trumpets for revival in our gathering for a reason. To bear witness that the day of the Lord will come as a thief in the night, and the Son of God will ride down to earth on the cloud with power, and the blast of the Shofar will be deafening, and the elect will be gathered. The era of repentance will be over and judgment will set in.

Every moment is an opportunity to drink from the water of grace, and check if we're in tune with God. The

Feast of the Trumpets is one of the appointed times of the Lord that gives us opportunity to reflect about our place in eternity. We found that the more you abide in the Father, the deeper He abides in you and shows you revelations of Himself.

CREATIVE HEALING: REVIVED FROM COMA

In the course of 2 years, we have seen God restore people from coma, mental illnesses disappeared, cancer disappearing. One of the most dumbfounding cases was a man who was on life support. His sister worshipped at LightHill with us. The doctors found blood in her colon and after a series of tests, they suggested she goes for a procedure to ensure it was not colon cancer. The night before the, she called. As we were about to begin prayers on the phone, my husband said the Lord said to him, "don't pray, worship me". We all worshipped, for about 15 minutes. The Lord said it was done. The next day, the sister called us to say when she got to her doctor, they did not find traces of blood anymore, despite two previous tests showing blood.

Because of this encounter, this sister said, well, you guys better bring my brother before God too. He is on life support and the doctors told the family to make end-of-life preparations. Shockingly, the sister said, "This is a perfect candidate for the next miracle". We said to God; Lord, you heard our sister. We called her up to pray over the phone, and I heard the Lord say, "I need someone who has an authority in his life to stand for him in my presence". Then I asked the sister, "Is your brother married"? She said no. Then he asked, is his mother alive? She said yes. He spoke to the mother, encouraging the mother to pray along. The next day, the sister called my wife. We told her the Lord wants a person of authority in the brother's life to stand for him before God. The sister said, "oh maybe that would be the son who is a young adult. The son had been saying he wanted his father to just depart after seeing what the father was going through". The power of words!!! This was when he came to the understanding that someone who had spiritual influence in the brother's life was wishing he would die, and the Lord wanted him to get rid of that pronouncement and nullify that. As we continued prayers that evening, the Lord showed me the image of two organs, with a pump in between. The Lord said, the pump was the cause of infection shutting down all other organs. The sister said it was the defibrillator used to keep him alive and the doctors were getting ready to take it off. The next day they took off the defibrillator and there was an unexpected turn around. Instead of dying, all the organs came back to life. That is one of the many of our encounters of Jesus, the Great Physician.

CREATIVE HEALING: DELIVERED FROM THE SPIRIT OF INSANITY

A lady was about to graduate college, the devil struck one month before her graduation. She went into a dangerous and aggressive mental state, and had been checked into a Psychiatric hospital in Virginia. We prayed with her relatives over the phone. The Lord said, bind and cast out a strange spirit. We did it instantly. The Lord said, she would be released on Monday. They called us on a Saturday, and the Lord said the release was on a Monday. I believed that report when the Lord said so, but to the canal mind, it would be unbelievable. In most advanced countries, severe psychiatric disorders accompanied with violent behavior necessitate rapid restriction of a person's freedom to prevent harm. The Lord also said to warn this lady to abstain from the kind of contents she was exposing her soul to. It turns out that they found on her phone graphic witchcraft images that she had been researching.

We bear witness to the availability of the raw power of God as in the days of old. Same power is available to people who will not compromise in their walk with the Lord. Same power is available to persons who become new in Christ, regardless of their old ways. Same authority is given to whoever will set themselves apart from the coolness and trends of this world and pursue the higher calling of holiness.

3

PROPHETIC INTERCESSION

Our assignments from the Lord are strategic. From interceding for America to interceding for people, nations, Churches and individuals. One thing that became very apparent is that God loves His people and no one can fathom the depth of God's love for mankind. Such love that The Lord sometimes raises up people you may never get to know about to intercede for you.

ISRAEL 2016 - PROPHECIES

"This is going to be a year that I will bring establishment to the nation of Israel. No longer shall the nation of Israel be a tenant on the land, I will bring establishment to the nation of Israel and I will eliminate all her foes, one after the other.

Fulfillment: In May 2018, this word came to fulfillment as the President Trump moved the United States embassy to Israel.

US PRESIDENTIAL ELECTION 2016 PROPHECIES

Prior to the election in 2016, The Lord said, "The Republican Presidential Candidate, Donald Trump is slowly moving towards the light. My people are praying for him and the result of the election will stun many. I will use him as a tool to correct America and bring many back to me". In one of our worship encounters, I heard the Lord say concerning America again:

"Haven't you seen America, that your teeth has been removed, although you put things in your mouth, you cannot chew, but I have come that I may restore you. O sleeping giant, I have come that I may restore you. How long will you go after other gods? How long will you go after other gods? Indeed, I have blessed you to be a blessings, what then will be when you depart from what I've called you to, I've called this nation a nation of givers, a protector of many nations, why then will u go back in the name of conformity? I have called you to fight for the ones not be able to fight for themselves, why then has the enemy deceived you into thinking you can do all these in your own strength? For the cry of the saints, I will restore you from the foundation up, and I will rebuild and I will make every broken wall, I will call your sons and daughter from afar off, and many shall come to your light. Arise and Shine, America Arise and shine.

I see a warrior who has received so many arrows but about to fall and die but kneeling with one knee on the ground and other knee is raised, but just as it's about to fall, strength just came. This warrior begins to rise, the Lord says He is going to raise America up again, He's going to fight for this nation. I saw a lot of people around this warrior, and they tied different types of thread to pull Him up, all these people were dressed in white robes, this is the prayers of the saint, if my people will rise up and contend for this nation. Do not give up on this nation of America. Pray for America.

The Lord says even the saints have come with a mentality that has come to plunder this nation. They have come to see what's in it without giving back, tell my children to repent and begin to contend for this nation. My children has a mentality that there is always another place to go back to, the Lord says when will you rise up and contend for this nation? When was this last time you wept over this nation? You keep thinking about how it will be well for your sons and daughter, but when will you fight for this nation? There are many believers even to cast the ballot but they just never do it. Then you complain about the status of the nation, the Lord says, what hypocrisy! It is easy to tear a thing down with word, when will you sit down, go on your knees and contend for America in prayers? The result of this election will surprise many and many will be forced to call my name, to run to my secret place, unless my people rise up and pray. Contend for this nation! Fight for this nation!

Beloved you need to pray. Pray that America will not implode, for a tiger from the East will try to take over. The Asian tiger from the East will try to take over but it comes with a lot of darkness. Yet people will be fed a lot of lies. It is the duty of the Church and the believers to pray. I see this Asian tiger has a lot of red, orange, white, black colors. Around it is a lot of darkness, I see this Asian tiger, wherever it goes it devours, it turns fertile lands to desert. Believers must pray that this nation will not be handed over even to the enemies. A star of deception shall rise from the East.

Warn my people, pray for America not to fall a prey to the star of deception that rises from the East. It is like a black hole that sucks in all the resources of my people. Stand in the gap to pray for the nation. For an imposter lion will rise up but it is merely a cat, it is not a true lion, it is not the lion of the tribe of Judah, green with envy against my people who will come with great deception, even to deceive" - Says the Spirit of God.

Since these words came out, we have not stopped praying for America and we implore you to join other brothers and sisters in crying to the Lord on behalf of America.

SINGAPORE PROPHECY - A KING THAT DOES NOT KNOW JOSEPH - AUGUST 2017

"Tell the saints of Singapore to intercede for the nation for the cup of wrath is about to unleash. Merry the prophets say, eat and drink they say, when I have not sent them. For calamity is about to fall upon the nation of Singapore. Tell the people to contend for the soul of that nation. For in the midst of merry-making lest not calamity begin to fall. It is not time to rest on your laurels Singapore. There is about to be a shift, a great undercurrent is about to build up into a big wave to spin into a revolution. Saints, go into intercession, so that a king who did not know Joseph wouldn't come into power".

Fulfillment: Barely a month after the Lord showed this revelation, we read in the New York Times headlines "Singapore Has a New President, No Election Needed".

SINGAPORE NOVEMBER 2017

"A turmoil is building underneath, the oppressed are

crying out to the Lord. Tell my people to rise and contend for the soul of that nation that the plan of the enemy will not come to pass over that nation. There are certain issues that will be brought into law in a couple of months. The children of God need to rise up in Singapore to pray. Tell the people to organize a prayer walk to guide the gates of that nation, for there are gates to the entrance of that nation. How can you my people put fire of on the roof and go to bed?. Arise, people of Singapore to pray. For I see where people were donating their earrings, made of gold and diamonds to melt together to create a golden idol. In a way, a national idol is being organized and built. Tell the people to arise and contend, for that nation is mine, says the Lord. If that nation falls to obscurity, there'll be a lot of imbalance in that region, tell believers to arise in prayers. I see people bringing up their earrings to put in the furnace to create a national idol. Tell believers to break in prayers. Woe to the prophets saying there is peace when there is no peace for they want to lead my people astray, tell the believers to pray now not give rest to their faces".

We really did not understand the meaning of the "national idol", we don't know what the specifics are, but we have learned to obey what the Lord says to us regardless of whether we can put a meaning to it or not. All we continue to do is to pray, and call our friends in Singapore to join us in prayers.

THE ZIMBABWE COUP

A brother had introduced us to his friends from Gambia. They wanted to seek our professional help for a technology project for one of the potential candidates for Zimbabwe presidential election, as the election season got nearer. This small group of Patriotic Zimbabweans was going to hire us for a technology project. As with any other project that we embark on in the marketplace, we seek the face of the Lord before any project.

As we prayed about the potential Zimbabwe project, I heard the Lord speak clearly and He said:

NOVEMBER 11, 2017 - PROPHECY FOR ZIMBABWE

"Something groundbreaking is about to happen. Tell them to go and get ready. Something great is about to happen in the nation of Zimbabwe. With the jawbone, ill scatter the enemy. There's a new chapter to the story of that nation and it is just getting scattered, so that you'll know the Lord can deliver by many or little.. He has broken the gates of brass and cut the bars of iron asunder. They need to pray so that a military coup does not happen"

Even when it did not appear so, there was nothing on the news; we began to pray against a coup in Zimbabwe. We were going to be hired as Technology consultants, and God was saying to us that change was coming but we should pray against a coup. How were we to tell our potential clients to pray against a coup? The opportunity came, and we told our potential clients to continue to pray for their country. We continued to pray for His will to be done. This was on a Sunday. On Tuesday we received a phone call from the contact person from Zimbabwe that it looks like there is a coup happening, but there is nothing on the Internet or in the news. A few hours later, the rumors began to flow, and some said it was a coup, some called it house arrest - one thing was clear, it was the end of President's Mugabe's rule.

NOVEMBER 16, 2017 VISION ON ZIMBABWE

Two days later, I saw a vision that goes thus:

> "I saw an iron fist. Zimbabwe is about to slip into the hands of a more difficult leader because of the way they are handling things. Witchcraft is at play, unless the people rise up and pray things will slip out. They have talked for too long. It is a season to arise and pray. I was reminded of the situation of the son of Solomon, where the kingdom was splitted into two. The Lord said to me, this is about to unfold. They are about to split into a higher hand; the kingdom will split into 2 which will send them back into many years of slavery. I am seeking the righteous, but there is no one to contend for Zimbabwe. I am seeking for just a soul to contend, but no one, for the prophet of Baal are dining and eating at the table of jezebel. let the people rise. It is not a season of

talking, a season of going down into deep intercession and prayers. There's a God who is asking for the faithfulness of the people. Let your mercy speak for the nation of Zimbabwe. Concerning the Christians in the nation, for you are neither hot nor cold for I will spit you out. Amend your ways. If the people will not rise, whatever they think is hard already will be worse. Tell the people, for the priest are seated at the table and eating at the feet of Jezebel. Let there be a great awakening. If the beloved will not arise, I see a cup. I see a white substance like pap, I heard the word "corn starch" and the I hear the Lord say cornstarch will be a food for the rich the way things are turning around. People need to arise; it is not an issue of words, but one of prayers. People need to arise. Call for a national day of fasting.

I also saw a man who wore a cap, like a military hat, but blow the hat is like a cap divided into 2, the first portion is like military, the other one is like a cap you wear on a native *attire and I saw a guy looking away and wearing this hat"*.

Fulfilment: I did not understand the vision of the man in a divided hat with one side military and the other side civilian until November 24, 2017 when a new administration was sworn in. The new President is a civilian while his Vice president is a retired general. It became clear to me that God was showing all these secrets not for us to have only the information, but to also intercede for nations of the world.

VISION ON EUROPE & UNITED KINGDOM - DECEMBER 25, 2017

I heard the Lord say; " The Prime Minister of the United Kingdom needs to take caution so that the kingdom will not be turned away from you into the hands of your neighbor. There is going to be a big shift in the United Kingdom as a whole. The carpet wall be slid off the feet of the rulers. There is still a remnant that will not bow to Baal, and the Lord will show mercy on His remnant.

Fulfillment: The Brexit - an ongoing debate about withdrawal of the United Kingdom from the European union continued to flood the news.

PROPHECY ON PRESIDENT TRUMP TO GAIN FURTHER POPULARITY IN - 2018

"Many will say 2018, is the removal of President Trump is here, it will not happen because the assignment of my servant is not over - says the spirit of the Lord. In fact, He will gain a further majority, preparing him for the next election year. The Lord says - I am gathering momentum for this country to be able to break the bounds of iniquity. To restore the ancient landmarks, for those who do not understand history will not understand inheritance, those who don't understand inheritance will be unequally yoked to rising issues of gender equality. Pray for President Trump, that the enemy will not use his health to ruin the nation. Because of the things he has been chosen to do, to steer the nation away from the path of iniquity, I have averted destruction and he has changed the history of America, says the spirit of the Lord. The prayers of the saints and their worship will continue to break the spirit of iniquity upon this nation. Believers need to continue to dedicate the nation back to the Lord. Concerning President Trump, warn my people not to be a part of where they talk evil of the president, for I have established this presidency and I am a God of justice."

PROPHECY JANUARY 2018, 2017 PRESIDENT TRUMP, US & ECONOMY

"The economy will rise in multiple digits and the country will know economic growth. Major restructuring is coming to the social security program in 2018 that will shake a lot of people out of their comfort zone and cause them to rise up".

Fulfillment: Interestingly, we began to see how the Lord was dealing with people who spoke ill of the president. Regardless of our opinions or disagreements, we need to be careful about what we say about our leaders. The best thing we can do is pray for them.

DECEMBER 21, 2017 VISION ON CATHOLICISM

I saw a lot of buildings collapse. The foundations of many buildings collapsed. I saw a church building and the arc to the entrance broke. I asked the Lord what this meant; He said something major will hit Rome in 2018. The seat of Catholic Diocese will bring a lot to the open. If believers are not careful, the exposure will erode the value of Christianity that may bring negative impacts. The Church needs to rise up in prayers.

Fulfillment: We began to see a lot of things come out in the open in 2018.

VISION ON AMERICA - MARCH 16, 2018

I saw the president of Russia. He was put in place as Egypt - a rod of discipline for America. The same way Egypt served as the rod of disciple for Israel back in the days. It was put in place as a discipline rod against America. I heard the Lord say, "If the nation would turn around its current course and seek the Lord with a whole heart, the impending invasion will be averted, otherwise Russia will invade America. Some trusts in Chariots, but in the name of the Lord, we shall conquer all. Raise an army of Spiritual warriors, intercessors that will bring the matters of this nation before me and pull down the stronghold. I'm looking for who will stand for this nation. It is not about the military power that she has, it is because of the decree of the Lord. Two major areas the attack will hit first, the national grid; disabling power across America, it will hit communication. And this will in turn, as a ripple effect, hit the financial market and the economy. That is why the Liberal agenda is very dangerous. People need to go back and retrieve the mantle of the Fathers, where people actually knelt down in prayers to stand on behalf of their nations".

PRAY FOR PRESIDENT TRUMP & AMERICA - NOVEMBER 2018

Starting from November 2018, the Lord called us into urgent prayers for America. He said the soul of America is sick and the spirit of complacency has taken over those who once tarried in prayers for America. The Lord said the nation has set its path on a decline, and if care is not taken, America will not become recognizable in the next 10 years.

The spirit of Pharaoh is out to draw blood. Pray for the President's health. Satan's plan is to cut short the assignment before the appointed time. Believers thought they have overcome since President Trump won the election and have gone to sleep when the momentum of darkness is gathering. Christians must arise for there is a great conspiracy of darkness under way. This is targeted towards 2020. There is a great campaign on going. That campaign is to make Christians run into hiding. Whoever comes in after President Trump is going to be so far left. There is a secret conspiracy going on, believers cannot afford to continue to sleep. Those ministers calling wrong right, calling right, some of them will meet with untimely death if they don't repent. A lot of them will go into hiding and a lot will conform. There will be tougher laws that make it difficult to call upon the Lord of Jesus. They will try to remove the name of Jesus from Christianity so that they can merge Christianity with Mormon, Catholicism and all sorts.

This should not happen under the watch of the Church and Intercessors. Pray for revival. Let there be a great awakening, a shaking and a cry to heaven to put out of business every function of darkness and manipulation of darkness.

SYRIA WILL CRY HOSANNA

I saw a map with the name of Jesus on a donkey in Syria. In yet a little while, Syria will cry out Hosanna to the Lord. Syria will enter into the name of Jesus. This is not by chance; it is the Lord rode on a donkey through the Middle East. There was a moving icon of Jesus riding a donkey moved through Eastern Syria into a country close to Syria. We pray for Syria - we pray that the power of the Lord permeates that region.

RAISING UP PROPHETIC INTERCESSORS

Beyond a shadow of doubt, God is raising up passionate warriors for His end time mission. Men and women, young and old from all nations who would tarry in worship and prayers regardless of what the world says. There are a lot of these types of urgent assignments that the

Lord has for His this generation. They are dear to God's heart, and we need to respond. People with a heart of compassion and love, that have covenanted themselves to the worship of YHWH are needed to stand as forerunners. These people also need to pray for access into the prophetic to get an insider access to the revelation of Jesus. The prophetic enables them to listen to the voice of God and stir up Daniel, Moses and Esther moments where they will take their place in the counsel of the Lord on behalf of nations and individuals.

The question is, will you allow God to raise you up as His prophetic intercessor? For some, all you need to do is to say to God, Lord - enroll me in your move, and then pay the price and walk the walk. It is a life-long walk of purity, faith, worship and prayers. Some men and women, some popular, some unknown have responded to that call. Their obedience has set generations free, and because of them, many people like Abigail and I came to know Jesus, and encouraged to walk into our calls.

4

THE EARLY CHURCH IN NIGERIA

The most addictive movies are not necessarily crafted by the best of the best movie makers but done with those who have a better understanding of storytelling. Every story has a purpose. Some stories are designed to encourage, to make one feel bad, to indoctrinate, to introduce beliefs. This is what the media has used very well to their advantage to the detriment of the Church. Stories have been put out there against the Church, to force people into doubting the existence of God. The enemy has mastered this and is currently using this against the Nigerian Church to shift the mindset of people. The current state of the Nigerian Church is not close to how the Church started. The enemy fought so hard against the establishment of the Church in Nigeria. The Church may go through a season of persecution, but the good news is that the Church cannot be eroded away.

Similar to Daniel's story discussed in later chapters is the story of a missionary and Bishop from Nigeria, Samuel Ajayi Crowther. He was taken into slavery when he was 13 years old. He was resold a couple of times until he finally ended up in the hands of Portuguese slave masters. The ship that was transporting Bishop Crowther was intercepted by the British navy's anti-slave trade patrol that rescued him. Little did the Bishop know that God had a grand design for his life. He ended up in Sierra Leone where he said "Yes" to Jesus and became a follower of Jesus. The Lord brought Bishop into a phase of deep learning of the Scriptures and he became a mission teacher, a Linguist and the first Anglican Bishop in Africa.

He worked with another great missionary of the 1800s, Reverend Henry Townsend. The word of God was translated into Yoruba language through the mission works of Bishop Ajayi Crowther. The divine Townsend - Ajayi collaboration produced powerful Yoruba hymns and made way for the first Church to stand on the soil of Nigeria in Abeokuta. The duo organized and translated the Scriptural teachings into local and consumable languages so that the gospel could reach and settle in our ends of the world.

The Church Mission Society (CMS) that Ajayi was a

part of simplified Yoruba writings. Bishop Ajayi helped standardize the writings of many Yoruba dialects into a single Yoruba language. Because of the unified language, communication was accessible to many fragmented dialects, and they united as Yorubas.

WHY AJAYI CROWTHER?

Here is why in Crowther's words;

> "About the third year of my liberation from the slavery of man, I was convinced of another worse state of slavery, namely, that of sin and Satan. It pleased the Lord to open my heart ·.. I was admitted into the visible Church of Christ here on earth as a soldier to fight manfully under his banner against our spiritual enemies".

Ajayi Crowther was a true son of the Nigerian soil. His background matched the qualifications needed to fight darkness. He understood the only culture. He had the understanding of the worship of the pagan gods and the rituals. He was a descendant of king Abiodun whose son is the founder of the current Oyo town. He was not gullible into thinking idolatry was culture. He knew better. The King of kings had to take him out of idolatry into slavery for him to meet with the Lord.

Crowther gave his life to Christ in captivity. He was baptized with fire and received his apostolic anointing as a captive.. Crowther's anointing was a rare breed. He broke the colonial limitations in a time where slave trade brought prosperity to economies of nations. Even when people didn't catch the vision and when Africans refused to help. Oppositions rose up against him from Africa and Europe. He set up the framework of the Church by the help of the Sierra Leone team who had no understanding of local languages. These were possibly some of the friends he met in his time in captivity.

He carried the Peter anointing. Bishop Crowther bore a special emblem on his forehead which reads the words in Matthew 16:18 "And I tell you, you are Peter, and on this rock I will build my Church, and the gates of hell shall not prevail against it." No other person had this authority. Not the earlier Portuguese Catholic missionary who attempted to build the first Church in Benin. The Benin gods roared at them and they fled. Bishop Ajayi and Rev Townsend were conquered by the power of the Holy Spirit. Such missions are only possible to accomplish by vessels that carry the live fire of the Holy Spirit. In them, there is a constant flow of high voltage power of the Holy Spirit that brings instant death upon any power that seeks to hinder the works of YHWH. Bishop Samuel Ajayi Crowther has the authority to open the seal on the scroll that had the secrets to breaking the spiritual strongholds over Nigeria in his days.

Throughout history, major breakthroughs even in the area of technology and science have been preceded by revival. Revivals are preceded by times of oppression, and when the people seek God intently, the Kingdom of God comes down to earth. The blessings brought by the establishment of the first Church in Badagry were numerous and still linger on today. Major victories followed Bishop Crowther's works. Language barrier was crushed. The print media kicked off. There were breakthroughs in the spheres of communication and journalism. While Christianity had been around since the 15th century, the Church was successfully planted in Nigeria in 1842.

When we remember the ministerial works of Bishop Ajayi Crowther, we must also remember that there are many others unreturned slaves who never made it back to their fatherland free. Notable descendants of slaves are Pastor Martin Luther King Jnr and Rosa Parks; two civil rights activists who fought for the freedom many now enjoy in the United States.

THE CHURCH: A CATALYST TO NIGERIA'S INDEPENDENCE

Biological and spiritual seeds of Bishop Samuel Ajayi Crowther continued the Father's work where the great Bishop left off before he went on to rest in glory. About 118 years later after the Church was seated on the shores of Nigeria, the freedom of one slave translated into the freedom of the entire nation from colonial masters. His mission opened the door to the independence of Nigeria.

Sacrifice, service and leadership have always been part of the Crowther DNA. After the Church had been planted. The move of God was headed into the government. God moved into the sphere of government and education. During the later years of Bishop Ajayi Crowther, new

Churches sprang up with the goal of making the Church as native as possible. They didn't want to continue with the culture of the foreign missionaries. The localization part of it was a good idea; it was one of the very reasons why the Lord chose Bishop Ajayi Crowther in the first place. The problem with some of the newly established native Churches is that some of their elders went back into idolatry and secret cults.

HERBERT MACAULAY: A SEED OF CROWTHER

Thomas Babington Macaulay was a priest and an educator who married Abigail Crowther, the daughter of Bishop Crowther. He was the founder of the prestigious and premier secondary school in Nigeria, CMS Grammar School, Lagos. Thomas Macaulay was the father of Dr. Olayinka Herbert Macaulay, the father of Nigerian Nationalism. I strongly believe Crowther's mantle was upon Herbert Macaulay who took the mission into the arena of politics. He also excelled in the realm of journalism, as he co-founded the Nigerian Daily News in the early 1900s. Dr. Herbert Macaulay was the founder of NNDP, the first Nigerian Political Party and he later founded the National Council of Nigeria and the Cameroons (NCNC), which produced Nigeria's first President, Dr. Nnamdi Azikiwe.

APOSTLE JOSEPH AYO BABALOLA

The great Apostle and Prophet, Joseph Babalola was the first spiritual son whom I believe to have picked up Bishop Ajayi Crowther's cloak. Apostle Babalola's parents were members of the Anglican Church. His father was an elder in the Anglican Church. His brother was a Sunday school teacher in the same Church. Ajayi's mission, "to fight manfully under his banner against our spiritual enemies" stays true to the missions of other God's generals recorded in history. Servants of God like Smith Wigglesworth, Martin Luther, John Wesley, Lester Sumrall, Derek Prince, Billy Graham and many others who God used to shatter darkness.

One of the roles of the Church is to influence the society by providing spiritual leadership. There's no doubt that the Church in Nigeria established spiritual leadership from its inception and became a pioneer in Education, Language, Media and Government.

BIAFRA: GOD'S PLAN FOR NIGERIA THROUGH THE TRIBE OF THE EAST - THE IGBO TRIBE

Moses was sent ahead of the Israelites into Pharaoh's palace when he was barely six months old. God appointed him as the deliverer of Israel from slavery. Moses attempted to begin his assignment earlier than the appointed time.

Exodus 2:11-15

> Now it came to pass in those days, when Moses was grown, that he went out to his brethren and looked at their burdens. And he saw an Egyptian beating a Hebrew, one of his brethren. So he looked this way and that way, and when he saw no one, he killed the Egyptian and hid him in the sand. And when he went out the second day, behold, two Hebrew men were fighting, and he said to the one who did the wrong, "Why are you striking your companion?" Then he said, "Who made you a prince and a judge over us? Do you intend to kill me as you killed the Egyptian?" So Moses feared and said, "Surely this thing is known!" When Pharaoh heard of this matter, he sought to kill Moses. But Moses fled from the face of Pharaoh and dwelt in the land of Midian; and he sat down by a well.

Moses tried to enter into the assignment God called him into ahead of his time. He tried to be the mediator but didn't understand the function of correct timing. He had the heart of a Shepherd and felt the pain of a father. Like Moses, anyone who gets into an assignment at the wrong time will fail woefully. Moses' inability to estimate his timing sent him into exile.

For every tribe in Israel, there is a different purpose. For the tribe of Judah is praise, and the tribe of Issachar is specificity. The men of the tribe of Issachar have the understanding of times and seasons, and knew the course the nation needed to take. There is a tribe in Nigeria made as part of Nigeria for a strong reason - The Igbos. The Igbo tribe has been given the anointing of money multiplication and the understanding of trade. Back in the days, the fire of the Holy Ghost did not permeate the region because Catholicism was the dominant religion. Hence, the regional powers misrepresented the Igbo identity to other tribes in Nigeria, sponsored confusion against them and raised up their fellow countrymen as their enemies. In 1967, the gates of Nigeria were flung open for the Igbo tribe to break off into a nation called "Biafra". God allowed Biafra to last for only 3 years. Biafra tells the story of the missing piece of Nigeria's thwarted economic development.

The destiny of Nigeria is to abide together; otherwise Nigeria would not have a voice without the Igbos. Although the effect of the break away led the nation into a civil war, God was fully involved and had His plans. There was a brilliant Yoruba leader who was instrumental to the fall of Biafra - Chief Obafemi Awolowo. The Lord wanted to use Chief Awolowo for a divine purpose of bringing together the nation, but he thought He could do it without the Lord. The Lord sent people like Prophet Ayo Babalola to him to speak to his destiny. The Lord reached out to Chief Awolowo to turn to him otherwise he would be snuffed out of the assignment that awaited him. The Scriptures say "Knowledge puffs up", there was a seed of pride in his origin, which eventually caught up with him - thinking a name was everything. Awolowo was an Economist with exceptional brilliance. He had the spirit of counsel after the order of Ahithophel, King David's counselor. General Ojukwu - Nigeria's military leader of the breakaway Biafra, gave him insider access to the plan for Biafra. Awolowo understood Biafra's strengths and weaknesses, and he advised the government accordingly. Awolowo solved the enigma of how to bring dissolve Biafra and bring back Nigeria - "cut supplies of food" and "give the Igbos 20 pounds to start afresh". That worked, but millions of children and adults died of starvation. The cry of the poor and needy and starved children reached out to the Lord. The Lord is a Just God - there was no way such an atrocity would go scot-free. The Lord wanted to use Awolowo differently if he humbled himself and came to the Lord, but he didn't. He never made it to the presidency despite many promises and expectations.

The Igbos would have been able to establish something great from the breakout, but the timing was wrong. Inside Ojukwu was a destiny crying out to break away from mediocrity, but the Lord wanted him and the Igbo people to channel their giftings rightly, as builders of the nation. These were the people who would be the driving force for the growth of Nigeria. They couldn't because the region was heavily involved in Catholicism when all they needed was the apostolic fire of the Holy Spirit to break fallow grounds and help build Nigeria's economy. The Igbos probably would have gone into complacency if Biafra were successful after their existence, rejoicing in their ability to accomplish a break-free at the time. The Lord used that event to create something else in the lives of the Igbos. They became extremely industrious and their hard work was blessed, making it safe to call them the Jews of Africa. The

Lord heard the cries of the Igbo and He transformed their mindset from that of oppression and deposited the spirit of entrepreneurship in them. The Igbos became a purpose-driven people. They understood what it means to lose an inheritance overnight and that it is possible for any government of the day to take away their money. A lot of them do not trust the banking system, they diversify funds and resources, and you see them carry a lot of cash.

After the civil war, more fragmentation came. That is why the Igbo industrialization kicked off after the civil war. Abba became like a China inside Nigeria, manufacturing electronics, shoes and all sorts of consumer products. They are gifted and crafters. The Bezaleel anointing was released upon an entire tribe. The Igbos are a gifted group of people. They are the Jews of the black nation. That's why when you see an Igbo person working for someone in a place, he's working with the mindset to save money and start his own business someday.

There is a spirit at work in the Yoruba camp, it is the spirit of complacency. The Yorubas have strong educational values, many are required to advance in their academics, and as a result, the educational values tend to overshadow the complacency spirit in the background. For a handful of people who have defeated this spirit, there are the manifestations, not in the multitude of their words but in the fulfillment of their God-given assignment. However, for those who have not uncovered this spirit, it is mostly covered up with excessive boasting, laziness, and extravagance. These are some of the spirits setting back this camp. This spirit is to be defeated by shaking away laziness and breaking the yoke of the spirit of complacency.

The Igbos were not so much into education but entrepreneurial. That shifted eventually because they realized there's nothing that could crown their success and they adopted education.

The Yorubas became more educated because of missionary influence. The missionary held education as a carrot to the rabbit, tightly put together. Education and faith was offered together. That's why you'll see more professors rising from places like Ekiti where premium is placed on higher educational accomplishments. Once the Igbos saw what people like Awolowo did, they were made strong believers in the values of education, knowing education will give them a voice. Education with the mindset of a lazy man does not go far. That's why you see the few educated Igbos doing it with passion. They went all the way, mixing education with industrialism - taking them to the long realm.

The Lord wants Nigeria to be unified. The strength of that nation relies on the unity of the nation. More so, the Lord wanted to use the oppressed - the Eastern Nigeria as a vehicle for the growth of Nigeria. If the Igbos had been separated from Nigeria at the time, the remaining portion of Nigeria might have gone back into slavery. There would have been massive influx of colonial masters touting in to help, but they would have brought them back into slavery. It was the Lord's master plan to keep Nigeria together for a greater glory.

The Hausas became very complacent because of the shift of power. They are the most laid back because of the high level of illiteracy rates. Without education, the Yorubas would have been considered the most laid back. Reason being that you find Yoruba as the least entrepreneurial of all the tribes. The Hausas became less entrepreneurial because of their location and the landmass. Their entrepreneurial mindset is not totally eroded. Hausas are still in touch with their cattle and animals. They still have to deal with the animals, multiply the number of animals and create milk. Almost every family needs to nurture animals. What further set the northerners back is the religion that they held unto - Islam. It fostered radicalism and all sorts of mediocrity.

BIAFRA: THE CHURCH AS A CHANNEL OF RELIEF

Beyond setting the spiritual direction for a nation, the Church is called to support the oppressed and the cast-away in times of need. The Church had a great sense of responsibility towards humanitarian efforts and disaster relief during the Biafra war. Countless numbers of victims of starvation were supported by the coalition of international Churches and local Church leaders.

"In spite of opposition and threats by the Nigerian Government the Church Relief Organization stepped up their airlift of relief in an attempt to match the growing starvation in Biafra. Starving Biafran children were flown out in their thousands to feeding camps in Gabon. On 9th December, 1968, Joint Church Aid decided at a meeting in Sandefjord,

Norway, to continue their nightly airlift of relief to Uli from Sao Tome which was previously interrupted by the Nigerian Government".

The question we need to be asking today is; does today's Church still have the capacity to function as a relief organization to victims of disaster? Is the Church running programs to influence the nation and the people positively? What authority does the Church have over sectors of the economy today? Is the Church raising anti-abortion and anti-gay prayer taskforce? We must begin to ask God to show us how He wants us to be a part of His move in cleansing nations through the Church. We cannot be a Church without impact; we must return to the Antioch model - the Church was sent out to deliver the message without compromise or fear.

5

THE GATES OF NIGERIA

Gates are the spiritual entrances holding the keys to a nation. The gates are the key entrances into Nigeria. There are 7 major seals in the 7 major landmarks of Nigeria. Those seals are the gates of Nigeria. These 7 seals are the main gates of Nigeria. There are also 6 minor seals; these are the minor gates of Nigeria. The major seals are the airports and the minor seals are the seaports.

They are Nigeria's international airports: Akanu Ibiam International Airport in Enugu, Kaduna International Airport in Kaduna, Mallam Aminu Kano International Airport in Kano, Murtala Muhammed International Airport Lagos,. Port Harcourt International Airport in Port Harcourt, Sadiq Abubakar III International Airport in Sokoto and Nnamdi Azikiwe International Airport, Abuja.

There are 6 other entry points into Nigeria. These are the minor gates. They are the sea ports; Lagos Port Complex, Tin Can Island Port, Calabar Port, Rivers Port Complex, Delta Port and Onne Port. In total, there are 13 entry points into Nigeria.

THE SEAL OF RETROGRESSION

We see the instances of angels as gatekeepers over cities in the Bible. One classic example is in Revelation 21:12: "It had a great, high wall with twelve gates, and with twelve angels at the gates. On the gates were written the names of the twelve tribes of Israel".

What comes into Nigeria and goes out through those gates are of great significance in the spiritual realm to Nigeria and Nigerians - home and abroad. The gates of the nation have been compromised. The departure of the Holy Spirit from the gates of the nation marked the time when the Spirit of God left. Whenever sin abounds, you will never find the Holy Spirit.

Ephesians 4:30
"Do not grieve the Holy Spirit by whom you were sealed for the day of redemption.

The seal of destruction was placed upon Nigeria in 1976 when evil was invited into Nigeria. The seal of destruction holds the secrets into the retrogression that the nation has faced since then. The 7 seals in the 7 major landmarks of Nigeria are referred to as the gates of Nigeria in the Spiritual realm. As the Church looked on, idols were imported into Nigeria. The seal of the nation was broken. The problem with that was that the power of God departed from the gates because the Church compromised, leaving room of heavy demonic penetration and infestation into the nation.

NIGERIA FALL: FESTAC 77 PICTURED FROM JUDAH'S LIFE

Nigeria is undergoing the most dangerous destiny perversion and defilement of the century. We can visualize Nigeria's fall through the experience of Judah in Genesis 38. Take a look at the crisis of Nigeria captured between Genesis 38 from verse 13 through 26. Tamar, the daughter-in-law, gets information that her father-in-law is coming to town. She goes on to take out her real identity and covers herself with a veil. She positions herself in open sight where Judah would not miss her. What motivated Tamar's actions? She was vengeful because she had not been given in marriage to Judah's third son as promised. Then Judah walked by and he thought she was a prostitute and went in to negotiate. In verse 16, a demonic transaction took place. Judah said to his daughter-in-law who was disguised as a prostitute, "let me come in". She obliged and demanded a payment. Judah lacked understanding of the cost of his destiny. He could not put a measure to the value of his own destiny that he asked the harlot, "what pledge shall I give you?" in verse 18. She knew what she wanted and demanded accordingly. She requests for the signet, a cord and staff in the hand of Judah.

The evil powers behind Tamar's action had seen the future of Judah as a God's lawgiver and the one who carries the scepter. The enemy came for three most important things that represented the glorious destiny of Judah. The staff - also known as a scepter is an ornament held by royals as a symbol of authority. The signet is a symbol of power. The cord is a symbol of bond signifying an agreement.

Like Judah, Nigeria has a powerful role to fulfill. Nigeria went into destruction when she opened the gates of the land to Satan during the Festac 77 event. "The children gather wood, the fathers kindle the fire and the women knead dough, to make cakes for the queen of heaven; and they pour out drink offerings to other gods, that they may provoke Me to anger" (Jeremiah 7:18).

There are angels appointed by the Lord to city gates of any city dedicated to the Lord. The seal of destruction was placed upon Nigeria in the year 1976 when evil was invited to Nigeria. This seal of destruction holds the secret to the retrogression the nation has faced since then. Anything will easily flow into the land because the guardian angels have been grieved and departed. The lives of the dwellers of the land are at risk except the dwellers that are marked with the seal of God as the untouchables.

Culture is one of the hardest concepts to define because you cannot lock down its dynamism. Thankfully, you can narrow culture down when you look into the interests, beliefs, values, and codes of a group of people. The devil has brought confusion to culture, and created his remixed version and tagged it using diverse phrases such as "cultural appropriation", "culture of the land", "culture of the elders". The Pharisees said to Jesus, "Why do your followers not obey the traditions we have from our great leaders who lived long ago"? (Matthew 15:2). And Jesus answered, "And why do you refuse to obey God's command so that you can follow those traditions you have"? (Matthew 15:3).

THE CLASH OF THE CULTURES

There is God's command and there is the culture of the elders. Africa is big on culture and tradition. We must zoom into some cultures and have understanding of the true meanings of those practices. There are cultures of the Kingdom, and there are cultures of the elders. The two cultures are parallel, and have nothing in common. Witchcraft has been carefully wrapped and presented back to the average church goer as culture

In times of worship sessions, the Lord gave us a revelation: The spirit of the Lord said, " There are major paintings that were given to Nigeria as gifts. There were also paintings given internally between different kingdoms in Nigeria". We had to begin research on the word of God that came to us, and here's what we found:

> "The opening ceremony of the festival took place on 15 January 1977 inside the National Stadium, Surulere, Lagos. One of the highlights of the ceremony was a parade of participants representing 48 countries marching past visiting dignitaries, diplomats and the Nigerian Head of State, Olusegun Obasanjo. Some participants in the parade wore

colourful ceremonial robes, some men were on 14-foot stilts, and Nigerian dancers carried flaming urns on their heads. To symbolize the freedom and unity of Black peoples 1,000 pigeons were released; a shango priest also set the festival bowl aflame.

"Following the successful completion of the festival, the artifacts of the 59 countries and communities were kept in trust by Nigeria, the host country. This prompted the establishment of the Center for Black and African Arts and Civilization (CBAAC), a federal parastatal with offices in Marina, Lagos and FCT, Abuja. Monuments of the festival are currently being preserved in a museum at the center."

Nigeria openly defiled God by importing idols into the country and that was the year iniquity entered into Nigeria. Demonic birds were released into the clouds of Nigeria; a pagan priest was brought in to perform fire rituals. Rituals as the name describes is a series of ongoing actions typically in a prescribed frequency by the receiving entity, and in this case Satan. Yahweh warned Noah to tell His descendants to stay away from the consumption of blood because the life of an animal is in the blood. When the laws were given to Moses, animal blood was some of the pathways to atonement for specific sins. That was why the blood of Jesus was the only blood that could atone for the sins of as many who believe in their hearts and confess with their mouth Jesus as Lord and Savior. Satan uses the demonic template of his knowledge of the blood sacrifice laws to oppress many. Majority of the death cases in Nigeria are unnatural deaths, these are blood of people sacrificed on the altars of Baal. Satan has hijacked control over the gates of Nigeria, he has infiltrated the country with witchcrafts activities which continue to require all forms of blood sacrifices.

The spiritual implication is that the country has withdrawn herself from the hands and care of the YHWH, and has been submitted to the forces of darkness. The Festac 77 event was a public rejection of the Lordship and the government of Jesus with demonic exchange sealed with the release of demonic birds released into the Nigerian airspace. The enemy presented this ritual as a cultural event and sold it to as many as believed, including the Church. The message of Jesus tells us otherwise, the Lord said in Matthew 24:28, "For wherever the carcass is, there the eagles will be gathered together. Yet we keep wondering why the number of deaths are reaching its highs, what about the demonic birds, the rituals, the prayers of Satan's priest who led the event?

The Church needs to rise up, rededicate the nation back to YHWH, and build powerful worship and prayer altars all over Nigeria before the country will move forward.

6

THE AMERICAN INFLUENCE

The ministries of some famous American preachers have influenced certain ministries in Nigeria. This is the origin of the theme; *"you can have what you want, with a focus on prosperity"*. Since African nations were poor, the message of change was welcomed forgetting that every Church has its timeline with God.

This is an influence where ministers deviate from the identity of Jesus and apply the "Sodom and Gomorrah" methods as in the ministries of some famous preachers. Some Nigerians ministries have become minimalists when it comes to their version of gospel. They don't deal with the demons; they have reduced worship to entertainment and noise. What manner of gospel that? Definitely not of Jesus.

The gospel of Jesus is a location-sensitive one. The Lord said He was not sent to everyone but to the lost sheep of Israel. He also made an exemption for the Canaanite woman who humbled herself before him. Jesus did not modify the gospel to fit into the Canaanite standards.

Entertainment, fanfare, pole dancing, and all manner of degradation have become the driving force of some mega ministries in America today. Witchcraft has opened a lot of branches in local churches and that's why people hardly encounter spiritual blessing and continue to die in silence. By the time they take a look at their lives 20 years into the future, they will find that they remain in the same spot or worse off than you were before your salvation story began.

The American Church is divided on the subject of abortion. Only the Charismatic movement seems to be fighting for the truth. Others just throw the conversation under the table. Yet some Nigerian ministries are copying this model. When a person says, "women should be free to choose whether to abort a fetus or not", think witchcraft. Witchcraft demands constant blood sacrifice, and what better way to get supplies of blood sacrifice than to murder unborn babies and say it's not murder? We are encountering a lot of church goers who are patronizing psychic stores conveniently located in American shopping malls due to the lack of the power of the Holy Spirit in most Churches.

Only rural America seems to be preserving Godly values right now. The metropolitan and cosmopolitan have lost directions. A lot of plurality has come into place. Christians have forgotten their roots. Like a pinhole camera with too many holes, there is overexposure that has given too much light. So is the dilution of the core value of the Scriptures. Unfortunately, the global audience does not see rural America. The global audience does not see rural America, but only see metropolitan America and copy their style of Christianity. The type of Christianity that does not believe in tongue-speaking or deliverance. The character of the founding fathers of America is being eroded by demonic influence because the Church is looking on and doing less. People of God need to wake up and intercede for the nation.

We don't have to go the way of the modern day Sauls who no longer have access to the voice of the Lord and can no longer make any impact for the Church of God here on earth. Yahweh wants His mission delivered as is, unfiltered, untainted, just the way He gives us the task, including the delivery of His word.

SIMPLICITY OF THE GOSPEL

When Jesus was speaking to some, He spoke in parables for the purpose of them not understanding because it has not been given to them to understand. To others, the message was clear and very simple. He gave them parallels, used stories to introduce the concept of what He's talking about. And He'll ask them questions. In breaking down the parable of the Good Samaritan, he used a story.

Luke 10:29-37

But he, wanting to justify himself, said to Jesus, "And who is my neighbor?" Then Jesus answered and said: "A certain *man* went down from Jerusalem to Jericho, and fell among thieves, who stripped him of his clothing, wounded *him*, and departed, leaving *him* half dead. Now by chance a certain priest came down that road. And when he saw him, he passed by on the other side. Likewise a Levite, when he arrived at the place, came and looked, and passed by on the other side. But a certain Samaritan, as he journeyed, came where he was. And when he saw him, he had compassion. So he went to *him* and bandaged his wounds, pouring on oil and wine; and he set him on his own animal, brought him to an inn, and took care of him. On the next day, when he departed, he took out two denarii, gave *them* to the innkeeper, and said to him, 'Take care of him; and whatever more you spend, when I come again, I will repay you.' So which of these three do you think was neighbor to him who fell among the thieves?". And he said, "He who showed mercy on him." Then Jesus said to him, "Go and do likewise."

This story is widely known across the world today. In the Yoruba communities in Nigeria, if anyone is overly nice, they call them "alaanu samaria" - which means "the merciful one from Samaria".

There is great spiritual blessing and fire in the simplicity of the message of the earlier missionaries who came to preach the gospel in Nigeria. The old missionaries who brought Christianity into Africa worked extensively on localizing the gospel to facilitate the delivery of the message in its simplicity. A lot of the simple stories used to pass across the gospel was rooted in language barriers. Some of these individuals who designed those stories were coming from the point that , "these people may not understand our complex English", and out of the lack of proper words to get to native speakers to pass the message, they said, "let's convey the message using a story book model", and it worked. In that simplicity was the hand of God and the gospel reached the hearts of people. Is not the word of God actually very simple? Of course it is. In the simplification of the message was fire.

These simple stories were the ones that caught fire causing massive revivals in African regions. Without knowing that it is the simple messages that catch fire. And that's why you find the crusades of Evangelist Bonnke become a ground of harvest for hundreds of thousands of souls. The power of the Holy Ghost moves in simplicity and the originality of the word of God. The simple stories of the Bible delivered the way it catches the fire. And you fail to see similar turnouts and conversations in western countries because the word of God is made complex.

If we take the gospel "as is", and cease being opinionated about the Scripture, tides will change and we will encounter massive harvests like never before. The weight of the flesh cannot carry the power of God. That is why the flesh seeks to protest against the word of God. The word of God is given to change our stony hearts into hearts of obedience.

The message and concept of the gospel is very simple. These kinds of record-breaking revivals are lacking in America today. The missing point is that the concept of the things that worked in Africa will work everywhere. The reason there are less miracles and revivals in western countries are the add-ons: the high level embellishment that ministers mix with the gospel thereby losing the core of the message of the gospel.

Sometimes, ministers go places like India and Africa, and preach simple messages. Some people refer to these preachers as simpletons. While they keep the core of the message simple, the God of wonders does wonders in building massive revivals; those who are supposed to be intellectually mature and capable don't experience miracles. The point here is to stick to the simplicity of the core message of the gospel.

POLLUTION IN THE AMERICAN CHURCH

The pollution you see today in the Nigerian Church was exported from western cultures and largely the American Church. The gospel came into Nigeria through missionaries, how else would the devil creep into the Church if not through similar channels?

When Noah worshipped the Lord after the flood, the aroma of his worship was delightful to the Lord and God established a covenant with Noah, his descendants.

Genesis 9:11-15

I establish my covenant with you: Never again will all life be destroyed by the waters of a flood; never again will there be a flood to destroy the earth." And God said, "This is the sign of the covenant I am making between me and you and every living creature with you, a covenant for all generations to come: I have set my rainbow in the clouds, and it will be the sign of the covenant between me and the earth. Whenever I bring clouds over the earth and the rainbow appears in the clouds,

I will remember my covenant between me and you and all living creatures of every kind. Never again will the waters become a flood to destroy all life.

After this promise, history has never recorded any destruction of the entire human race despite the fact that humans continue to exhibit wickedness like the days of old.

America is known to have exported iniquities to nations of the world in recent times. The homosexual agenda and all sorts of iniquity have been exported into nations of the world from America. The White House was lit up in colors of rainbow to rejoice when the Supreme Court ruled in favor of same-sex marriage. President Obama responded that justice had arrived for the same-sex community "like a thunderbolt".

"Yet even in countries where legal protections have improved, like Brazil and Argentina, it's difficult to draw a straight line between U.S. advocacy and progress, and in Latin America, those changes have been accompanied by increasing violence against LGBTQ people. In Uganda, a court eventually invalidated an anti-gay law the U.S. had emphatically opposed. But in Gambia, anti-gay rhetoric has escalated despite a U.S. decision to revoke the country's preferential trade status following an LGBTQ crackdown".

The rainbow belongs to God and is a sign of His covenant. He gave half the rainbow to us for our remembrance of His promise and as a pact. The rainbow is sacred, and in John's vision of heaven in Revelation 4:3 where he saw he saw that the rainbow was indeed a circle, around the throne of God. As we have seen, only half of the rainbow, the other part is in heaven, as shown to John. How then can a nation allow the symbol of God's covenant be turn into a token of homosexual pride?

In the American Church today, iniquity is on increase. Divorce rates, gay marriages, violent crimes rates are up. There are pastors who are unable to speak up against abortion. As if that was not bad enough, there are also pastors who go with the stance "If a baby, a fetus is not a life, then why restrict it?" Yet, some Nigerian pastors have modeled their Church structure after these pastors. These are ministries today bringing in pole dancers to Churches as part of their worship, turning the Church into a strip club.

In some Churches, a lady cannot be part of the usher if they do not fit into certain clothes size, as if they were clubhouse hostesses, making suggestive prescriptions on how they want their ladies to dress in order to attract people to Church. We are seeing this trend in some of the Nigerian Churches today. The ushers are on a parade every Sunday to welcome the gentlemen to Church.

These trends have changed the narratives of the Nigerian Church and have significantly impacted the spiritual growth of the average believer. Since a lot of new generation Churches are modeling some of these demonic trends from certain American ministries, the power of the Holy Ghost is lacking in those Churches. This is the major reason why the massive harvest of souls during evangelistic crusades seems which were once promising becomes unsustainable in the longer term. And the cycle repeats itself. Take for example, an international evangelist comes to Nigeria and 3 million people accept Jesus. How many churches can we safely lead them to for proper spiritual nurturing? Majority of those who filled those salvation cards have no spirit-filled Church to help them grow spiritually, hence falling back into false religion.

In the next chapter, we see the influence of the modernized American Church on the Nigerian Church.

7

THE ATMOSPHERE OF THE CHURCH AFTER 1976

If the church realigns to the core message of Jesus, the body of Christ would harvest souls exponentially. At the beginning of our intercessory ministry, one of the earliest words the Lord spoke through His prophet, my husband, was that "people were going in their droves to hell, straight from the church". As a first generation believer in Jesus, that word stood out to me for reasons I share below.

As a former muslim, I learned early at Quranic schools about heaven and hell. From those lessons, I learned how terrible it would be to end up in hell. The fear of hell and afterlife gripped me and I resolved in my heart I did not want to be in a place outside of heaven when I die. We were taught about self-righteousness. Hence, I would not be open to an individual who was dressed half naked preach Christ to me.

First encounters with the gospel came in the early 1990s from the ministries of Mount Zion and Christ for all nations. In these ministries, I saw the beauty and authenticity of Jesus, and the seed of the gospel was sown. The 1990s was also a time where many churches were getting into the trade of modernizing the gospel. This sent confusing signals, especially to me, at a time where I was considering accepting Jesus. With this experience, I have no doubt that here are many muslims out there today, who have been appointed to inherit salvation, but are held back because of the misrepresentation of Jesus right from the pulpits. If you are one of such persons, I say to you - through life-altering rare signs and wonders that I have seen in our personal lives and while ministering to others, I bear witness that Jesus Christ is the Savior and the Son of the Living God. Through the revelation that has been given to me from the studies of the Scripture, I bear witness that Jesus is the Living Word of God. Because of the level of God's move in our worship encounters, I testify that Jesus Christ is the Lord of lords and King of kings. Beyond every reasonable doubt, the Son of God died, arose and went up to heaven. He sent to us the Holy Spirit and in His name Jesus, there's tremendous power, and in His name is the utmost protection.

As a former devout Muslim, some of the roadblocks to my salvation were mainly churchgoers who identified as Christians. In my moments of considering Jesus, I looked up to those Christians around me as models of Jesus. A lot of those people who I spoke to had no understanding of their faith. Some of them identified as Christians because it was the faith their parents passed down to them. That was not an acceptable response to me. I needed proof that Jesus is Lord. My soul was important to me and I would not allow anyone who didn't know what they were doing convince me to hand over my soul to a god they did not know. Little did I know that I was not looking for mere words, but encounters, testimonies and the demonstration of the power of the kingdom of God. That explains why those my soul was not won by Christians who lived like pagans. I would not trust them with my soul.

I answered the first altar call in 2001, but like many who had gone astray, I returned to the Lord in 2014, my walk with Jesus has been followed by an explosion of the tangible power promised as promised in Luke 10:19 - Behold, I give unto you *power* to tread on serpents and scorpions, and over all the *power* of the enemy: and nothing shall by any means hurt you. Not just that, I have the greatest companion, the person of the Holy Spirit who answers all questions.

I would safely say that the Church is operating way below its spiritual authority. With Jesus, the possibilities are endless.

THE MANTLE OF THE FATHERS

In a revelation, the Lord spoke about a mantle which He called the Mantle of the Fathers. The mantle of the fathers is the experience of similar anointing powers that was present in the lives of the earlier prophets, teachers and evangelists. The mantle still rests on a few fathers; the Lord has given me the privilege of identifying a few of them: The Mantle of Apostle Babalola was distributed to select men of God across the nation: There are thousands of God's true servants who have gone and who still live. They have contended for revivals and the move of God across Nigeria. Some of them have remained nameless and faceless while the Lord has brought some to the public glare.

In the vision, here are the men of God who had the mantle: The late ArchBishop Idahosa of Church of God Mission International, the late Prophet Obadare of Christ Apostolic Church, the late Prophet Samson Oladeji Akande of the Ede Mountain, Prophet Olowere of CAC, Oke Agbara, General Overseer and Pastor E.A Adeboye (The Redeemed Christian Church of God [RCCG]), Dr. D.K. Olukoya of Mountain of Fire and Ministries (MFM), Bishop David Oyedepo of Faith Tabernacle, Prophet Hezekiah Oladeji of

CAC Canaanland, Bishop Francis Wale Oke of Sword of the Spirit ministries.

My personal encounters with God in some of these ministries founded by some of the men of God listed above are discussed below starting from CAC founded by Apostle Ayo Babalola.

CHRIST APOSTOLIC CHURCH ENCOUNTERS

In my journey through the Church in Nigeria, I passed through CAC from birth to about age 5, I was the youngest in my grandmother's CAC choir. I would follow grandma and the choir to sing in Ushi-Ekiti, Iyin-Ekiti, Go-go Ekiti. Our choir group was very popular. We were invited to every major event in the surrounding neighborhoods especially the funerals. My instruments of worship were rhythm sticks. When I beat the sticks together, it produced sounds -- {ko ko ko ko ko]. There was no other little kid around, and my companions were the older grandmas in the choir. This helped me gain a deep understanding of the Ekiti dialect. When I moved out of Ekiti to be with my mother, people laughed at my Ekiti accent. My childhood in CAC exposed me to songs of the spirits and unceasing prayers.

FOURSQUARE ENCOUNTERS

Although Foursquare church was not founded by any of the servants of God listed above, there are powerful encounters to share. Then our family moved to Foursquare Church. In the children's Church, we were once taken out to evangelize and we had the privilege to preach to an old man who was a Muslim. The old man seemed quite interested in our message. Two weeks later, we followed up to check on the old man to see how he was doing and to remind him of the gospel. When we knocked at his door, we were told that he no longer lived there. The next week, my late grandmother and I were returning from the Church. We saw a wake-keeping going on. And I peeped at the photo of the departed, lo and behold, it was the old man we preached to that was gone. The people at his house did not tell us he had gone because they thought we were too little to understand. The Foursquare branch we attended was heavily invested in children. During one of our outreaches, our destination was Ipetu-Ijesha. A community was heavily infested with chickenpox. There was a man in charge of the youths. He led us to Ipetu-Ijesha townsquare where we had an open-air crusade. It was indeed a center of rituals. We saw all forms of leftover foods and bones at the location that had been used for sacrifice. When we got there, our Pastor stepped on the altar. His body began to itch. The man of God who took us on the mission called forth the power of God radically and the itching stopped. He also authoritatively decreed an end to chickenpox outbreak in that town before we left. In my little heart, I was full of joy and happy to be associated with Jesus. Foursquare Church's four-dimensional message was Jesus the Savior, the Baptizer, the Healer, and the Coming

King. As young children, that message stuck to us and we carried it wherever we went.

REDEEMED CHRISTIAN CHURCH OF GOD ENCOUNTERS UNDER PASTOR ENOCH A ADEBOYE: AN APOSTLE OF CHURCH BUILDING AND NIGERIA'S PASTOR

During my teenage years, I joined RCCG when someone invited me that they were searching for a Keyboardist. In my time at RCCG, the Word and discipleship were the core of the ministry and the events were tagged "Let's go fishing", "Digging deep". Our General Overseer was and is still Pastor E.A Adeboye, a torchbearer, and anointed to continue the works of Bishop Crowther in the realms of Church planting, a national mobilizer. An influential kingmaker sent to pastor government leaders. Under Pastor Adeboye's leadership, the Redeemed Christian Church of God has grown into a global ministry of more than 196 branches worldwide. The G.O. is a spiritual father to many and he is known for his simplicity and humility. Wherever you see G.O., you see his wife, Pastor (Mrs.) Folu Adeboye, next to him. Growing up in Nigeria, I served on the worship team in a local RCCG branch where I was a Piano musician. Pastor Adeboye's ministry was the nurture of Christian faith in my earlier years.

DR. OLUKOYA: A PROPHETIC GENERAL WITH A

MANTLE OF POWER - GENERAL OVERSEER OF MOUNTAIN OF FIRE AND MINISTRIES

My next 12 years outside of Nigeria in Singapore were years of spiritual lukewarmness and rebellion. They were years when I "worshipped" God from afar. It was also the years of directing worship concerts and building worship teams. In those years, the raw power of the God that was a part of my childhood seemed far away.

I have encountered God in the ministry of Dr. Olukoya as an adult. An uncompromising man of God. My wife and I attended one of the branches of MFM in the United States for 3 months. Dr. Olukoya carries the mantle of power. In a dream, I saw him listed as a General under a family tree that belonged to the Christ Apostolic Church. He is an unusual prophet of God. He carries the spiritual DNAs of the fire prophet Elijah, Bishop Crowther and Apostle Ayo Babalola. A man of explosive prayers, Dr. Olukoya teaches spiritual warfare from Jesus perspective. He calls it a DIY ministry, where he teaches believers to roll up their sleeves to spiritually destroy our dangerous adversary before he gets the first mover advantage. This prayer model was exemplified first by Jesus, the Son of the God when He taught the disciples about the different layers of casting out of demons. Jesus pointed out to his seemingly frustrated disciples whose words didn't get a demon out of its hiding place. He told his disciples, "And he said unto them, this kind can come forth by nothing, but by prayer and fasting" Mark 9:29. God found Him as the right person to reach that

81

population. He had the right background for a strategic assignment. To confound the wisdom of the wise, God is using Dr. Olukoya as a Scientist Scholar to reach many including the modern-day educated Christian who has lost touch with the reality of the idols of the land.

BISHOP DAVID OYEDEPO: A GIANT OF FAITH & A LEADER WITH THE KINGMAKER ANOINTING - PRESIDING BISHOP OF FAITH TABERNACLE

Bishop Oyedepo, the founder of Faith Tabernacle is one of God's servants who carried the mantle into the realms of education and business. He has the mantle of a vision-caster and kingmaker. The Bishop is anointed to raise "next-in-line leaders". Through educational establishments such as Covenant University, Bishop Oyedepo has been used to bring improvements to higher learning in Nigeria.

The Lord showed me a 6-year paradigm vision. In there, I saw a man wearing a green and white "agbada". When I looked at the man's face, it was President Buhari's face, but when I looked at the body, it was the body of an opponent. The man in the agbada hugged Bishop Oyedepo. I heard the Bishop saying, if you can only loan me the country for six years, I will transform it. He said six years is what it takes to transform the country". I asked the Lord to explain the meaning of the vision. The Lord said, the farm boy who rose to the position of the kingmaker. The Lord translated this vision as an adaptable model and time frame for building excellent projects. From nation building to personal development, the 6-year model is usable across all areas of life. People can go from level zero to attain their goals in 6 years. 4-years is what it takes to build excellently and the other 2 years is for the change to become visible. Bishop Oyedepo has profound insights and keys that can turn Nigeria around.

EVANGELIST REINHARD BONNKE: AN EVANGELIST OF FIRE SENT TO AFRICA

Part of my teenage years was spent volunteering when CFAN came to our city. I am thankful to Adonai, for making me be a part of this movement of His power.

If those who have been led to Christ through the Evangelistic Ministry of the great Salvation Missionary Reinhard Bonnke were a nation, they could form a nation almost as populous as Germany. Christ For All Nations is recorded to have led 78 million people to Christ over 44 years of Evangelist Bonnke's leadership. Making it the biggest harvest of souls for the Kingdom of Heaven recorded in our times.

Bonnke's ministry reached the neglected and unreached group of people in areas under heavy spiritual lockdown - the disco club, Islamic regions in remote and urban cities in Africa. Signs and wonders followed gospel campaigns, the blind saw, the dead raised and new babies received. Evangelist Bonnke's ministry eventually became a friend to Africa, despite several roadblocks along the way.

PROPHET HEZEKIAH OLADEJI: THE PROPHET WHOSE ANOINTING BROUGHT ME A GREAT AWAKENING

Prophet Hezekiah was one of the few people who gave me hope of the authenticity of Jesus as the Lord and Savior.

The Lord said He has raised His servant, Prophet Hezekiah for the following reasons: to restore holiness to the Church, sanitize the body of Christ, build up the walls of Nigeria through the Church, work as a the Refiners' fire of the Lord and teach transgressors thy ways of the Lord.

The Lord has raised His servant to restore the ways of the Lord in the CAC, and bring oneness to a divided fold.

HOW POWER LEFT THE CHURCH

There is still power in the source of the vision, rarely do you find power as the vision flows through the rivers. Power is no more in the Church because many who serve under the fathers of faith do not have revelation of the missions. Many do not want to build; they desire independence and want to start a Church not authorized by God. This is why there seem to be many Churches, yet less power and influence on the people and society. Material prosperity is part of the gospel but it is not the entirety of God's message. People have only caught a minute portion of it - financial prosperity and have forgotten that the most vital portion - the prosperity of the things of the kingdom of God. Spiritual and kingdom prosperity encompasses blessings in the spirit, soul and body. That was why the Lord told us to see first the Kingdom of God.

No doubt, the Church is in the era of financial prosperity for the reason of making reasonable impact for the kingdom. For the reason of prosperity, many unsaved souls are also running to the house of God as a result of the manifestation of prosperity they seek in their own lives. Many of these unsaved people lack the essence of the sacrifice of Jesus. They remain unsaved; yet seek prosperity from a God they have never surrendered The Nigerian Church has lost its potency to bear witness to Jesus. Rather than being the witness of Jesus, the Church has become the source of allegations against Jesus.

Acts 1:8 indicate power is a companion of the Holy Spirit. When the Holy Spirit comes in, He brings along power. "Power" talks about capacity, authority and influence. Spiritual power. Power also talks about ability, efficiency and might. The reason for the power is for the early Church to receive the capacity to function effectively it its primary purpose - being a witness to Jesus.

Another major shift began to happen in the Church after 1993 and the Church went into sleep after 1998. 1993 to 1998 was a period of spiritual unrest and spiritual fire where the Church gave no rest to God. There were different movements, different Churches. It was right after the year 1998, 1999 that a lot of copycat ministers rose up in Nigeria when there was a huge movement of copying the American Church and pollution entered. From that wave of desires lust of the eyes, world materialism, some had good intentions, some had no good intentions and came into the Church with pollution and powerlessness.

THE CHURCH'S EXODUS FROM THE WAY

As the demonic infested Churches, all the major government ministries that were once consecrated places of decision-making and policy-making became desecrated as well. The people in leadership in those government ministries are members of defiled Churches. Some of these leaders in government are friends of the pastors fleecing parishioners. The Church lost its spiritual authority at this point. The Church became a bad influence for the government as leaders in the government were taking cues from the Church leaders.

The massive amount of wealth being amassed by leaders in government sectors and Church leaders enticed a lot of people. Those who identified as Christian found their way to Churches in their droves because of the promise of wealth. A lot of them were not interested in the knowledge of God, but in the anticipated prosperity. As a result of this, the Church leaders gained large following and some of them acquired wealth at the expense of the congregation. The government had two choices; play along with the Church or place sanctions on the mode of operation of the Church. Since there is substantial corruption already in Nigeria's law system, the government could not do anything about it. The government of Churches is bigger than the government of the nation because of the numbers, turning the Church into a mighty political weapon. As a result of that it became a parasitical system; Church feeding on the government, the government feeding upon the Church.

There were actually few testimonies of people moving from poverty to wealth, but these testimonies were magnified which inspired many to run to Church. The Church became a huge machine for people cutting corners to get wealth. The people do not fear the God they claim to serve, nor be a living testimony to Jesus through their actions. There is nothing to reflect their association with Jesus, except their exceptional attendance records in Churches and their religion of greed.

This became a massive loophole in the Church and spiritual authority and power was completely lost. As the Church became prosperous, the devil created a sweet spot for himself and his agents in the Church. Witchcraft became more prevalent and began to thrive even more. Churches were turned into social gathering when societal groups brought the native dress codes (aso-ebi) into the Church to express taste, class and power. Practices that are deeply rooted in pagan worship spread like wildfire. Some Church leaders fled to the occult for power. There is a demonic league of pastors who are idol worshippers and cultists. As the spiritual void widened, there became a huge vacuum of spiritual power and because the enemy has ridiculed pastors, it gave rise to a very few truthful strong prayer organizations and different deliverance ministries.

MINISTRIES AND THEIR CLASSES
YOKE & BURDEN ALLEVIATION-CENTERED

CHURCH

The first segment is the "yoke and burden alleviation centered Church" There are a very few grounded ministers in this category. The remnant deliverance ministers in this class have a lot on their hands. There are only a few of the non-compromising anointed left in the area of spiritual warfare. They are not driven by money or given to worldly pleasures. They live in simplicity. These ministers flow along with the move of God, but some of them don't have a lot of time to teach the word deeply. They spend more time in running deliverance sessions and prayer meetings where people come to get delivered. This created a group of people who want a quick fix and turn these ministries into emergency rooms, just to rush in, get delivered and only to go and return to sin again. A good number of their deliverance candidates come from the other classes of Churches discussed below.

There arose a group of copycats again who needed to display false power but unwilling to go through the sacrifice. As that started, a different round of deliverance ministry started. The demonic ministers use occult powers to generate magic and show. The people fall under their captivity because they lack the knowledge of the word of God. People would believe anything, as long there's a physical manifestation. There you find promotion of white garment Churches just for a "quick fix". There is also a demonic display of power by demonic prophets. This goes back to people needing change and deliverance from works of darkness.

The Atmosphere of the Church After 1976

THE FEELING-BASED MOVEMENT

The other segment is a mixture of many things. It is the new wave. The feelings-based movement is where people put together music to exalt their emotions, without the proper grounding of the scripture. These types of ministries receive the toad and frog anointing where they only act out gymnastics, drama and make noise on the pulpit to drive emotions.

The feeling-based movements are the ones who have turned the supposed altars of YHWH, the True and Living God into an entertainment platform. They import artists and comedians who come to imitate the true worship of God on the stage. When God states that worship is conditional, " Those who worship me must worship me in truth and in spirit". How long will iniquity rob the Church of its glory? How long would you allow your mockery of YHWH send you into captivity?

The Church needs to go back to the deep foundation of the word, failing ministries needs to be retrained and refocused. A lot of GOs are not supposed to be GOs. They need to be taken into the depths of the word of God. A lot of founders of the feeling-based movements are talented musicians who have not been sent to plant a Church. Most of them have no tangible encounter with the Lord. How then can you tell people about a God that you have not encountered?

POVERTY-ALLEVIATION CENTERED CHURCH

The leading segment is the wealth-promising segment, called the "poverty alleviation centered Church. People are there mostly because there is a promise of prosperity, and the messages are focused on motivating and inspiring for success.

Some of the ministries in this class teach popular practical topics like Leadership, Time-management, Personal branding, Communication except the Kingdom of God, holiness and spiritual growth. The problem with this is that the new believer is stunted in growth, denied the propensity to explore the power of God available to believers and is focused after worldly pleasures neglecting the eternal and endless pleasure in the Kingdom of God.

Parties affiliated with this segment are quick to say they have a strong foundation in the word. That could be true, but would be a lie when the power of the word is made of no effect when the time comes to put it to use and the last resort is to visit the Yoke and Burden Alleviation Churches for a dose of quick deliverance.

BATTLE OF TONGUES AGAINST THE CHURCH

There have been a series of tongue attacks launched against the Nigerian Church in the past year or two from the pit of darkness especially on the subject of tithes and offering. That campaign was broadcasted from the pit of hell. It was made possible by the complacency of the Church and also by those who are fleecing the sheep and living affluently at the expense of the poor. Is not the gospel of Jesus one of truth that prospers in the realms of the spirit, soul and body? How then can we allow the gospel be tainted because of greed?

The divorce of Christianity from its Antioch roots has given a free pass to all sorts of heresy and powerlessness. It is time to return to our Jewish roots. Because the Church has buried her hands deep into iniquities, it became easier for Satan to attack the Church with mere words. The current battle right now against the Church is the battle of the tongues arising from complacency. The Church needs to repent and do what she has been called to do.

EXPANSION AND NEW CHURCH PLANTS

As at 2018, Nigeria has probably the highest number of church plants in the world. Popular ministries are expanding by planting new branches across the world. This is supposed to bring blessings and freedom to many nations of the world. Some of the Churches expanding to western countries like the United States and the UK are for divine reasons. One main reason is for the deliverance of groups of people who might have not been emancipated from spiritual slavery. The people whose forefathers were taken into slavery and never returned. The people who are tormented by the idols of their father's house back in an African village where they have never been. Then the Lord decides to send ministers with the heart of Daniel to them in the foreign land. Ministers who will go out to set free the captives. Some of the modern day General Overseers caught the vision, but a lot of ministers sent on foreign missions do not catch the vision. Nigerian ministers in the western countries have assignments in the ministry of deliverance. Unfortunately there are a lot who will neglect the rough work of expelling the demons and claim to have been called to be celebrity preachers. Generations are being held down because of this mentality. Everyone of the disciples were sent out to cast out the demons, and set the captives free. The ministry of Nigerian ministers is strategic in this area of deliverance because of their local knowledge of these dark powers. A lot of western churches have no revelation on the subject of deliverance or satanic modus operandi in the African communities. In moments of deliverance, we begin to see manifestation of local African demons in the lives of African Americans who are descendants of slaves. These demons and ancestral problems were passed from generations.

Wherever you see complacency, control, evil propaganda, and powerlessness in the Church - look no further, witchcraft has taken over. Majority of the chronic witchcraft cases the Lord has been bringing our way has its root in Africa. When traced down, it can be traced to the western part of Nigeria, and most times when we zoom in, it was from Nigeria, and neighboring countries. We see witchcraft manifest in all forms of way in the United States.

The question is; how can a Church selling entertainment come to the understanding that there is a local demon back in Africa tormenting a person in America?

To save them the trouble and tons of questioning, they ban the people from speaking in tongues and from any spiritual exercise that will open their eyes to the spirit of the Lord.

This is a strong reason why the devil is fiercely resisting Nigeria, and bewitching the missionaries sent abroad to deviate them from delivering enslaved groups of people. This is the reason why the devil is attacking Nigerian Church, so that many around the world remain in captivity. God wants to do a lot through Nigeria, but Satan saw this long ago and has been doing all its best to pervert the motivations of the local Church.

General Overseers and Senior Pastors who received the vision for the ministry from the Lord can apply the transition model used by Evangelist Bonnke. CFAN impacts nations globally, yet its offices and locations have been strategic hence the theme of the mission has stayed true to the mission. This model is usable for Church expansion and transition to incoming Church leaders. Without proper transition, the blessings that belong to one generation ends with that generation and there is no continuity.

THE CHURCH MUST STOP ENDORSING INIQUITY

"Church, take a stand. The Church is selling the seat of power to the highest bidder. Tell them to stop, tell them to stop endorsing iniquity to the highest bidder. Or else, they will be exposed in a whole new dimension. For what they are preparing to do, they are preparing for a military will to come back to Nigeria. This will be a punishment especially for the Church. Call the Church to rise up. Church rise up, and see the foolishness of your heart".

CHANGE IS COMING TO THE CHURCH

The Lord is bringing a change and uprooting individuals that are operating a profiteering ring from the Scripture instead of using the teachings of the Scripture for the edification and profiting of souls. "I, the Lord will arise and decree judgment starting from the Church". There are some Churches where believers and followers are empowered to follow the ways of the world and seek after fleeting pleasures of sin when they ought to be a channel to keep sinners out of iniquities.

SPIRITUAL FATHER AND SON/DAUGHTER RELATIONSHIP

The doctrine of spiritual father and son relationship is scriptural. Many have taken this doctrine out of Scriptural context. There is a place of order in God's house and a place of seeking godly counsel, mentoring and lessons. Some have taken the spiritual mentorship doctrine too far and have translated it into idolatry. There are cases of spiritual children worshipping their "father in the Lord", giving all the glory belonging to God to their spiritual dads. We see situations where some group of young ministers hardly get to know God or spend time with Him, but rely on spiritual mentors for all spiritual insights. When the Holy Spirit calls them into fasting and prayer, they hardly yield. On the other hand, when mentors summon a fasting, they respond. These are some of the practices the Lord is pointing at as reasons why His spirit has departed the lives of many. God is calling for a total repentance. He will never share His glory with anyone. If done right, the Lord sanctions the doctrine of spiritual fathers and children with Elijah and Elijah's relationship as a classic example to emulate.

EXPEL COMPROMISE

Compromise needs to be expelled from our ways. Set aside the Church for worship, prayer and word of truth - not entertainment or lies, regardless of the crowd size be it 100 or 1 million. Then we will see the glory of God return. Many who have previously lost direction will be restored, workers of iniquity will turn to Christ or be consumed, marriages will thrive, truth will be held in high honor, the people will experience God's love and healing will come. Whatever our missions are, the overall theme should lead to salvation, nothing more.

LOVE AND ELIMINATE LEGALISM

Love is the basis of our faith. We were saved by grace not by our works. The Lord wants us to eliminate legalism in all manners. Legalism seeks to control, seeks to impose over others, it seems to laud one's opinion over others. Legalism does not give grace. We must do away with all forms of legalism, and realize that the freedom bought for us at a price is not a license to sin. We are loved, and we must love too.

8

THE NIGERIAN YOUTH

There was a son wishing his father were dead so he could take over his inheritance. This young man had no regard for elders, no understanding of thankfulness; and was laced with the spirit of entitlement. Waiting for the father to die, and in his insolence, he summoned courage and spoke to his father, "daddy", "old man" or however he called his father, he probably said to his father, "I need my portion of the inheritance, since you are taking too long to die". *How could that be when the father is still alive? For a will to attain validity, death must have occurred, since it has no force or legal power as long as the one who made it is alive.-* Hebrews 9:17. Surprisingly, his father obliged and gave it to him. As if the father didn't know he knew he was going to squander it in the first place. This story of the prodigal son is similar to the current situation of the Nigerian youths who either have no humility, or put on the garment of false humility and are getting into political races just to go and cause more mess.

The Lord will promote a lot of the younger candidates running for office only if He finds true humility in their hearts.

EMULATING DAVID'S CULTURE OF HUMILITY AND HONOR

Leadership is cultivated from the heart. The mantle of leadership is passed onto the one with the contrite heart. Humility is one of God's major requirements for anyone who desires to lead others. The lack thereof is enmity against God. While we worshipped, the Lord said to us, "Tell them, there's no place in old age or leadership for anyone who exalts their hearts or disrespect elders under any condition". When King Saul was small in his own eyes, The Lord anointed Him as the commander-in-chief of Israel. When pride was found in Him, He was replaced with David. When the heart begins from the heart. When the heart is infested with pride, it ruins opportunities for leadership or strips leaders off their position.

When David was anointed as a replacement king Saul, he never walked over the fallen king. He humbly gave a helping hand to his boss. David became one of Saul's favorite armor-bearers that Saul didn't want David to be out of His team. David also ministered to his boss whenever evil spirits took over him.

While David rose through the ranks in Israel's army and won battles , Saul's became David's number 1 enemy. Envy and jealousy plagued the fallen king that he forgot that the Splendor of old men is their gray men and that the glory of young David was his strength. King Saul made numerous attempts to kill David, yet David failed to take the opportunities he had to kill his boss. He would not strike King Saul and kept close to his hearts the words of Psalm 105:15 - ``touch not my anointed and do my prophets no harm".

Leaders may have missed out on their duties or failed woefully at their jobs, we should never condemn them. Their authority comes from God. Some leaders are being used as vessels of blessings to the people they serve and some are being used as rods of correction to their communities. Whichever the case may be, God installs leaders as He wishes. Regardless of how the reign of a leader turns, we can influence the decision of that leader by speaking directly to God - not by talking down on the leader. It is easy for us to say if I were in their shoes, I'd do better. The truth is that - God listens and you will be given a chance to lead in some capacity. In most cases, performances do not turn out as anticipated. This is what happens to anyone in leadership without the spirit of God in their lives. No leader is able to make a positive impact on the nations without personal intimacy with the Lord.

The Lord spoke to us saying that the youth attempting to contest for the Nigerian elections will not get close because they are yet to understand the value of giving respect and honor. Those without respect for the elders would only create a culture of disrespect in the nations if given a chance in leadership.

DANIEL'S SPIRITUAL GENES

Many leaders inherit spiritual genes of those whom they have submitted to. Daniel studied deeply the prophecies of an older prophet Jeremiah. He inherited a portion of Jeremiah's spirit of prophecy and intercession.

Daniel was a teenager when he was taken into captivity in Babylon. Daniel was sent to the king's court in Babylon where he became a Prime Minister. The reign of a king who served a pagan god did not deter Daniel from submitting to the administration. Daniel understood the laws of his God. He observed the Levitical law by honoring his leaders, because he feared the Lord. (Leviticus 19:32) "You shall stand up before the gray head and honor the face of an old man, and you shall fear your God: I am the LORD."

He had no physical mentor, but he was an avid reader. There was no indication he ever met Jeremiah even though they were from the same country, but different regions. Daniel was from Judah and Jeremiah from Israel. He was able to reach leadership in the King's court because of his vast wealth of humility, wisdom and knowledge. He was able to see beyond what was available for the Israelites in captivity. He was a man who carried the mantle of intercession. Like every other person who moved in the deep power of God, Daniel's 21-day fast preceded breakthroughs in the region.

PROPHECIES TO THE NIGERIAN YOUTH

There's a generation of those who despise the elders. Those who the elders mean nothing to, not knowing that if you look at the rot of the Bamboo vessel, you will miss the diamond in the bamboo.

I heard the Lord say about the Nigerian youth:

PROPHECY: HONOR THE ELDERS

"Tell the youths who are running for elections without respecting the elders, they will never taste it unless they turn their ways around in repentance. For a nation that does not have respect or respect for elders are beckoning to death and digging their own grave. Tell them, it is time to put themselves in the shoes of their elders and rewrite the wrongs that the elders have written. The youth need to understand the mindset that was plaguing the elders, so that they can create a lasting change".

PROPHECY: STAY OUT OF ARROGANCE

"Warn my people. Arrogance has crept into the nation. The uncircumcised youth who is trying to take the reins of power knows nothing about governance and will make even more mess. It is not about the abundance of the persuasion of the heart of men. Many youths who are trying to become leaders will fail woefully. In their attempts of not accepting defeat, they'll form one great party and yet still be defeated. Where there is no honor of the elders, the Lord is absent. When a nation prides itself in being reckless in their heart, when honor is missing and not given to the ones in authority, failure occurs. It is a time to cleanse their own hearts, stop pointing fingers to the leaders. A nation that rejects its leaders will not see long life. Order and respect for those who have come before is the way to go."

RIGHTING THE WRONGS OF THE ELDERS

Some elders have the reputation of shutting down voices of truth that rise up against their lies. The young can effect change by giving firm insights and counsel to the elders in humility and love. Let humility enter into the core of your being and carry the laws of God in your heart, in your head and all over you. For without humility, there is no place in old age.

In the days of the Internet, talk has become so cheap and there is a rising group of keyboard warriors who would hurl insults at elders without giving it a second thought. If anyone delivers themselves from the sins of their ancestors and turns themselves away, all the sins shall be written off.

Romans 13:1-7
Let every soul be subject to the governing authorities. For there is no authority except from God, and God

appoints the authorities that exist. Therefore whoever resists the authority resists the ordinance of God, and those who resist will bring judgment on themselves. For rulers are not terrors to good works, but to evil. Do you want to be unafraid of authority? Do what is good, and you will have praise from the same. For he is God's minister to you for good. But if you do evil, be afraid; for he does not bear the sword in vain; for he is God's minister, an avenger to *execute* wrath on him who practices evil. Therefore *you* must be subject, not only because of wrath but also for conscience' sake. For because of this you also pay taxes, for they are God's ministers attending continually to this very thing. Render therefore to all their due: taxes to whom taxes *are due*, customs to whom customs, fear to whom fear, honor to whom honor.

The Lord's warning alarm continues to blow on the Nigerian youth. The Lord is calling for repentance and the embrace of a humble heart.

God hates pride and He is at war against the proud. God openly declared his hatred for the proud. When the Ark of Covenant was returned to Jerusalem. David gave up his reputation as king to worship God. He danced and exalted the name of the Lord. David returned home to bless his family. The Scripture records that Michal; the daughter of Saul despised the way David danced in her heart. It was what Lucifer did. When worship flowed through him, in his mind, he desired that worship would flow to him.

2 Samuel 6:12

> David said to Michal, "It was before the LORD, who chose me rather than your father or anyone from his house when he appointed me ruler over the LORD's people Israel--I will celebrate before the LORD -

Not knowing that anyone who despises or opposes the worship of YHWH is set up for destruction. When everyone in the house got a blessing, Michal received the curse of barrenness that night. It is time for every youth to get up and wear the garment of humility. Put yourself in the shoes of your elders to re-write the wrong that the elders have done. You have to understand the mindset of the elders so that you can create a lasting impact.

A NEW BREED YOUTH OF FIRE CARRIERS

There is a new breed of youth rising up, yearning to worship God, longing to hear from God and tarrying in prayers. The Lord is using them heavily as carriers of revival. They are well informed, technology-savvy and goal-driven. They are prophetic, intercessors with burden for nations, and are not ashamed to take the word of God to their campuses, or start a Bible Study group at their places of work and most importantly, they wear a royal robe called humility.

9

NIGERIANS IN DIASPORA

As the Lord brings us to many countries, we meet Nigerians in their droves. Many of us left Nigeria to study and some came to stay. Whatever our reasons were - we shared something in common; the memories of childhood in Nigeria. With some, we spoke the same local dialects or loved the same local foods. One undeniable truth is that Nigerians love their country. Once they step out of the shores of Nigeria, they seem to cherish the memories created in Nigeria.

After we began our ministry, our intercessions were initially focused on our dearly beloved America. A nation that welcomed us with open hands and ensured that she became home to us. We would pray for the government, for godly causes, leaders and America as a whole. Starting from 2017, the Lord spoke to us of the need to pray for Nigeria. He reminded us of Daniel in captivity and his sacrifices of prayers for Israel.

Israel went into captivity 70 years in Babylon. Daniel was a young boy when he was taken to captivity. Daniel didn't forget the God of Israel. He took The Living God into the government of a pagan God in Babylon. He carried the laws of God in his heart, and followed diligently. He researched Jeremiah's prophecy for the times and seasons. The knowledge gained from his research was used to estimate the duration of his country in captivity. He stood as an intercessor for Israel in a foreign land. Daniel "fasted, prayed and petitioned" God after 70 years had passed in captivity, and the Lord answered His prayers.

There are many Nigerians God assigned similar tasks as He did to Daniel. Two of such persons were Bishop Crowther and Reverend Townsend. These were missionaries who will take the worship of YHWH and His word unfiltered into the darkest places in Nigeria. God is calling many into that assignment today. Sons and daughters who will give counsel from the heart of the Father to leaders in government, and take the story of the Father's love to the unreached in inner cities and in the deep of Nigeria where fancy hotels and wifis have not reached. There are Nigerians whose tongues are anointed to set the captives free and heal the broken hearted on the streets of the nations of the world.

If you'll join us in praying that the time is ripe for them to remember Nigeria and place Nigeria on the top of their minds. Nigeria is far from the foundations that God laid through the hands of Bishop Ajayi Crowther and Reverend Henry Townsend. Nigerians in diaspora carry the

DNA of these two Diaspora missionaries. They have threaded similar realms. Flown across similar seas, educated similarly, learned other cultures, and share the same mission - the great commission. Where else to take the message of Jesus than our beloved Nigeria?

Until every Nigerian in diaspora, starting from us, makes a commitment in the nature of Psalm 137, they will not be able to walk truly in their inheritance regardless of where they are. Walking in the Psalm 137 commitment means putting an end to the orphan and escapist mentality that has stifled the growth of Nigeria. God indeed brought us out to work on us, so we can become a blessing to Nigeria in any capacity - spiritually, mentally or financially.

Who else would rebuild Nigeria if not us. If we're able to understand our inheritance and say, Lagos, Ibadan, Port Harcourt, Enugu, Abuja, Kaduna, Kano, Abia, Benin, Calabar, I will never forget you and begin to sow back to our beloved home the seeds of intercession. The current dark clouds looming over Nigeria will vanish.

You may not know how to start praying for Nigeria. You can start by saying to God, "Lord open your eyes, see the desolation of Nigeria and save Nigeria, have mercy and redeem Nigeria". As you pray, the Holy Spirit will teach you further how to pray for Nigeria. Remember, God doesn't need a multitude to change nations. He needs just one person. He used only Daniel. He used only Bishop Ajayi Crowther to enter uncharted territories. See this like the day the Lord called Abraham. He said, " Come to a place that I'll show you" For the obedience of Abraham, a nation was formed, and an entire nation of Israel was blessed.

The question is: Will you contend for Nigeria in prayer

10

THE 2019 PRESIDENTIAL ELECTION

The political climate and economy of Nigeria is buried in iniquity. People have seen iniquity as the way of life. The change has come. How many destinies have gone to waste? How many use their offices and leadership to commit adultery, shed blood and sacrifice to idols. Everything runs out, including grace except for the love of the Father. The Lord said to me, "don't you see there is an abundance of gifted people in the continent of Africa? What the enemy has taken away from the economy, I have blessed my people in all manner of gifting"

The 2019 election is going to be a one where the Lord uses the rod of men to correct a nation. Starting from the middle of 2017, the Lord began to show us what He is about to do in Nigeria. We have always taken prophecies as a conversation starter with God. Every time He speaks to us concerning what He is about to do in the life of a person or a nation, we take it back to Him in prayers.

God is seeking intercessors who will stand in the gap for Nigeria. It is urgent and time is running out. The prophecies below will give you an idea what God is set to do. We do not have to accept the words as our fate as a nation, because we can change His heart through repentance and prayers.

PROPHECY: THE SPIRIT OF AWOLOWO 2017

"The spirit of Awolowo is rising up again, where people try to govern with their intellect, but that does not work as well. There are parties being formed with his ideal that wants to bring back things from that era, but without the power of the Lord, there won't be any change in Nigeria. Nigeria needs the power of the Holy Spirit. The Southwest has an opportunity to be in power again. Another seed of Nnamdi Azikiwe is coming up. It appears that they teamed up with the seed of Awolowo or someone who embodies Awolowo, they'll team up to emerge as leaders, but they'll need the power of God to succeed, if they try to do it all on their own, it'll lead nowhere"

PROPHECY: THE MKO SEED, SEPTEMBER 22, 2017

" As political candidates begin to rise up in Nigeria. They

thought Donald Trump is nonsensical, because I needed a man who would say whatever I wanted to say. Concerning the political scene of Nigeria, the MKO seed is being raised up. The upcoming one shall be such an interesting one because the people are fed up. Divide they'll say but the nation will not be divided instead, the children of former political figures will step in".

We strongly believe the 2017 prophecies on the spirit of Awolowo have to do with the many young candidates running for election in 2019. We are of the opinion that the Lord has a leadership design over their lives, but a lot of them are driven by the spirit of intellectualism. This spirit is rooted in pride which hinders God's plan for them.

TIED TO THE THRONE - A PROPHECY ON PRESIDENT BUHARI'S PRESIDENCY & 2019 ELECTIONS

Humility is far from the hearts of many Nigerians. The Lord is set to do a new thing in the upcoming 2019 elections. The current president is tied tightly to the seat of the throne. Only the Church can unseat him. Because they have ridiculed him, the Lord, the Defender of the defenseless is defending the current President. Only the Church has the power to unseat him, but the Church is not ready. The Lord says, this leader has been spoken ill about and the Lord does not condone that. The Holy Lord does not sit down to behold injustice. The Lord has dethroned a kingmaker in Nigeria. For the gross injustice, and the war of words placed against President Buhari, the just God will not allow such injustice;

He has been given the power. The Lord is the deliverer of the oppressed.

I also heard the Lord say to me clearly, tell the people, "A decision has been made, I am the one who fights for the abused. I fight for the afflicted, for the oppressed. There is a certain individual that has been abused and talked about, for I have chosen Him. I will not allow the kingmakers to choose the new king. I have disgraced the power of the kingmakers. Some of them will fall into irrecoverable blunders. He who they taught could not perform will perform. He who they have ridiculed will perform. I am the one who has instituted the greyness of hair. Who amongst them can talk about the things of old? Those who do not understand the culture of honor will never come close to leadership. The nation will be purged again. There will be great unrest before the great calm".

After the election, I saw President Buhari sitting on a tree and he was looking down on people from the top of the tree. He was cutting branches from this tree to the heads of people on the ground. The people on the ground were Nigerians. The president forgot the branches he was cutting was from the tree he was sitting on. As he continued to cut, the tree grew weaker and he was about to fall, but the other trees around him didn't allow him to fall. I heard the Lord say there is going to be a time that the Lord will bring him through some lessons where wisdom will be released unto him.

MILITARY TAKEOVER: VISION CONCERNING

NIGERIA IN JULY 24, 2018.

While in worship, I saw a vision with the image of a man in full military regalia. I asked the Lord who this was; Tunde Idiagbon. The Lord said to me, the spirit of Tunde Idiagbon is coming back. There is a leader who is going to rise up to power in Nigeria with authority to shape up people. I saw this man in a ceremonial military outfit, as he disciplines people, he continues to smile. The Lord says, the military is coming back to Nigeria. It is almost a final decision in heaven.

When this military personality comes in, He will deal with the Church first. This is a situation where the Church is bringing judgment upon a nation, when the Church is supposed to be the protection of a nation. All sorts of Churches will be closed down, massive persecution will begin, people will be marched out of Churches, it will be a dance of shame and a situation where birds will go out to feed on the body of the people.

The Lord wants to purify the nation. It is through persecution that purification builds up. The Lord wants to move through Nigeria. God wants to use Nigeria to shine its light, and Nigeria needs to be purified. Believers are called to rise up in prayers, so this does not happen. If believers will not rise up to pray to avert this situation, It'll take another 14 years to get out of the military rule. People will be shocked for the first 7 years and the next 7 years will be spent on thinking of how to get the nation out.

In the vision, I saw people's hands tied and raised up, being matched on the streets, and people became calm and gentle, especially the Church, as a result of military discipline. There's going to be the heavy military presence and activities on the streets of Nigeria. The Lord said to me, "Tell the Church to pray! It is almost a final decision in heaven".

Another name the Lord mentioned to me during this encounter is Agunyi Ironsi, a past Nigerian leader. The Lord said, the spirits of Agunyi Ironsi and Tunde Idiagbon are rising back up. The factions of these past leaders will be split into two. One will be stationed in the North, one stationed in Lagos and they are going to be the two major powers. The Lord said, it will be a situation where regular programs will be interrupted and the same screen will go live all across the nation. It was not so much of a panic but an interruption of the regular TV programs across the nation. I saw Nigeria and her children became comfortless. The Lord said, "If I could only find 10 faithful servants of the Lord in that country", I will save the land. If I could find 10 faithful who have not bowed down to Baal, I will save the land.

Under this new alliance, the military will be beefed up in such a rapid way especially the air force and the navy. The Lord said to me, "Nigeria can be compared to a goat that has lost its shoes and complaining of being mocked".

Judgment is coming for the Churches, starting from Nigeria. He wants to purge the nation. Some ministers will take their own lives when things begin to unfold. In the vision, the Lord showed the image of a man who is supposed to be able to pass through a regular door but has grown out of proportion, and has his own entrance, which can no longer contain a regular man. I wondered what that meant, and the Holy Spirit said, " A lot of acclaimed "men of God" have elevated themselves. They have become unapproachable; the people are unable to approach them. They have put themselves so high up there. And they have said in their hearts, I'll make a dwelling for myself on the top of the mountain where people can see me. Those glass houses will be put down, says the spirit of the Lord.

VISION ABOUT REVOLUTIONARY BLOODSHED IN NIGERIA

I saw a lot of bloodshed in the coming election. It will be a revolutionary bloodbath. The young ones who are coming to declare such liberal views and opinions are coming with unconsecrated hearts and will only bring the nation to ruin. Like Solomon's son, Jeroboam who ruled with an iron fist. He ended up splitting the nation into two. I heard the Lord say, "Pray for the nation of Nigeria, as I am moving through the nation, a lot of voices that do not belong to the Lord, will try to rise up and simulate that they are from me. They are only moving forward to expand the left over agenda of sinful movements like homosexual and abortion movements exported from the Clintons and Obama rhetoric. It is in no way what I intend to do".

HUMILITY IS FAR FROM NIGERIA - NOVEMBER 13, 2018 VISION

I saw a massive sword over Nigeria. The nation is heading towards a divide. There are only two major factions right now. One is of the president and every other faction. There is a strong hold over the Presidency. The President has chained himself to the throne. The Lord said, "tell these young people to have an inclination for the elders. The Lord can do much by the hands of the youth. The Lord will not break His rules. If they can be respectful, they will get to the throne. If they are not, they will not get to the throne. As a result of the education of many, disrespect has crept into many hearts and is destroying a lot of them especially the Yoruba race. The wrong knowledge is destroying a lot of people. The official language of Nigeria needs to be humility. That nation must be known again for its humility. Humility is very far from Nigeria right now. Satan has entered and changed the rhetoric. Let the culture of Nigeria be that of respect for one another".

IMPENDING JUDGMENT COMING AGAINST NIGERIA VISION SEEN ON NOVEMBER 26, 2018

"Gatherings without God is emptiness. Nigeria is closer to the fist of the Lord that is being released. When the fist is released, there will be massive shakeup. Some people will fall out and some will fall into line. So that people can wake up to what He intends. It will be in different waves. If they listen, the nation will be transformed. If they don't more shakings will occur. A nation that despised the Lord is heading towards the endless pit. But if a nation realizes its errors and turns around, the Lord will avert the judgment. For the sake of what is about to happen in Nigeria. Don't stop praying for

Nigeria. For Nigeria is about to enter into a prophetic destiny but if intercessors do not arise to contend, there's no watchman to discern the time. The time to wake up for Nigeria is now".

JEHU: THE PRESIDENT NIGERIA NEEDS

Nigeria needs a Jehu-like president. A spirit-filled and disciplined man. Nigeria needs a disciplinarian who hears from God and will only execute based on what the Lord has spoken. A person who would cast down the stronghold of darkness and iniquity. A person who would lead the nation with the scepter of Jesus in one hand and the assignment of Nigeria in the other hand. A person like Jehu who goes forth to execute the words of YHWH without turning to the left or the right. A person who will destroy the spirit of Jezebel that has sat over the nation for decades, and a person who will restore order and lead the nation back to the Lord. This is the president Nigeria needs.

THE JUST, YET LOVING AND MERCIFUL GOD

God has created a supreme justice system, both for the righteous and unrighteous. He specializes in disgracing the counsel of the wicked. He is also the very ever-loving ever-faithful, everlasting God. He is the one who offers repentance to as many as will be humble. The Lord never brings shame or guilt. The image of God has been so perverted because of the image of some earthly fathers. It is difficult for people to see God as a God that is so good, kind and loving. Sometimes people see God as the all-strict God, like a God that people must tiptoe around. He is not. God is faithful to His word and never reneges on it. This is why He warns ahead so that His people can turn around from their wicked ways and walk into His original designs for their destinies.

11

HEALING & REBUILDING NIGERIA

The giant of Africa as she is fondly called, but what is a giant without power? What is an oil-rich country without the capacity to grease her own elbow or generate light for her sons and daughters? A nation whose manufacturing industry once thrived, and its glory squeezed away.   We have reflected a lot as a nation. We have analyzed the problem, talked about it, slept over it and even cried over it. Nigeria's problem is summarized in the Scripture below:

Deuteronomy 28:30-34

> You will be pledged to be married to a woman, but
> another will take her and rape her. You will build a
> house, but you will not live in it. You will plant a
> vineyard, but you will not even begin to enjoy its
> fruit. Your ox will be slaughtered before your eyes,
> but you will eat none of it. Your donkey will be
> forcibly taken from you and will not be returned.
> Your sheep will be given to your enemies, and no one
> will rescue them. Your sons and daughters will be
> given to another nation, and you will wear out your
> eyes watching for them day after day, powerless to
> lift a hand. A people that you do not know will eat
> what your land and labor produce, and you will have
> nothing but cruel oppression all your days.

As at 2018, Nigeria continues to be plagued by the
accessibility to basic infrastructure such as electric power,
quality education, clean water, healthcare, sanitation and so
on. The current state of Nigeria is the current spiritual state
of the Nigerian Church. Interestingly, the solution to
Nigeria's fundamental infrastructural problem is embedded
in the identity and description of the person of the Holy
Spirit.

The Scripture tells us that the Holy Spirit is the Spirit
of the Lord functioning across all domains of life. Fire and
power accompanies the Holy Spirit whenever He comes into
establishment in a place or a person. Counseling,

sanctification, and purification are also known as works of the Holy Spirit.

NIGERIA'S ELECTRICITY PROBLEM

It comes to a time when people are searching for answers and when nations are looking for solutions. Job was an embodiment of righteousness. He found himself in afflictions his righteousness was not supposed to earn him by human measures. He asked questions. God responded with the description of His magnificence.

Many are asking concerning Nigeria, "why don't we have stable electricity"? "Why is the government not solving the electricity problem"? Why is there no availability of clean water to the public? Why is there no healthcare access?, and the "whys" continue. There are encoded answers in the Scriptures. Let's explore together.

THE HOLY SPIRIT AS LIGHT

In 2013, on a flight to Dulles, the plane couldn't land as scheduled. No, there wasn't a traffic jam in the air, but the weather had gone bad. It was very foggy and landing was deemed unsafe. The pilots were waiting for increased visibility and also considering touchdown at nearby airports. I didn't like option number 2 - diverting to other airports. That would mean we needed to return to the airport to claim our luggage. Thankfully, we were cleared for landing after an extra 55 minutes in air.

A similar occurrence happened when the world was

being created. Everything - the earth, the seas was still in its raw form. No trees, no animals, no mankind or skyscrapers or yachts yet. And the Spirit of God hovered around. The Spirit did not land on earth. Then God brought in light by His words as explained in Genesis 1:1-3. This became the standard. Light must be brought forth for processes to continue. Take away light and processes come to a standstill. Our flight couldn't be cleared for landing because there was no sufficient light.

In the scientific context, Power is defined as "energy that is produced by mechanical, electrical, or other means and used to operate a device". Jesus explicitly warned his disciples not to depart from their primary location - Jerusalem without receiving the baptism of the Holy Spirit. He explains to them, "you shall receive power when the Holy Spirit comes upon you; and you shall be witnesses to me in Jerusalem, and in all Judea and Samaria, and to the end of the earth". Acts 1:8. In other words, the Holy Spirit will be their enabler in order to become witnesses of Jesus. They waited for the Spirit and received the power for their assignments. And the results?

One of the first results was that the disciples were enabled to do unthinkable things like speaking other languages that they were not trained in. The Holy Spirit brought light into dark areas of their mind, and they spoke eloquently in other languages. The Holy spirit brings light into darkness. Without light, most of what we currently have will not be usable. With light, processes become active and production continues, purposes are fulfilled.

The Spirit of God was present before light came. The

Spirit came to enable the words, "let there be light". And once there was light, there was power to continue the works of creation. Light is one of the presentations of the power of the Holy Spirit.

The Lord God got even further creative with light. He made variations of it. The greater light, He called "Day" or "Sun". The lesser one, "Night " or "Moon". Then he set up the control and timing parameters. The heavens must give light to the earth, and he created time out of light. Light is the framework of time. Time management is all about light. Your awareness of lighting will give you the urgency of time. The very backbone of everything is light. God made time function perfectly before putting the waters into its place, before creating lands, plants, trees, before the sun, moon, starts, animals and people. He created light first because without light the plants, man or everything else cannot work. No wonder that those who understand how light works understand videography, painting, the one who understands photography understands the concept of lighting, creative designers put light into perspectives, anyone who is able to master the use of light would perfect their craft. Those who understand light will understand that invisible doesn't mean invincible, not everything that hides itself from light is absence or unreal.

That's why the Light can be safely called The Spirit of Wisdom. Discoveries of light from the scriptures are mind blowing. God reveals in Job 38:15 that there is a permanent home where light resides and a dwelling of darkness. God pointed out in Job 38:19 that there is a way where light passes through and a route where darkness travels to reach the heavens at the required times. Science has verified the movement of light and gone further to measure the speed of light. In 1638, the great Galileo in his work *Two New Sciences* summarizes the Aristotelian position on the speed of light as:

> "Everyday experience shows that the propagation of light is instantaneous; for when we see a piece of artillery fired at great distance, the flash reaches our eyes without lapse of time; but the sound reaches the ear only after a noticeable interval." -

His conclusion aligns with the prophecy in Ezekiel 1:14 :

> "And the living creatures ran back and forth, in appearance like a flash of lighting".

We need to light up our homes at night and power up our devices. Electric power is needed to achieve these. Electricity is being generated in a lot of ways in 2018. A variety of renewable energy sources are used to generate electricity and were the source of about 17% of total U.S. electricity generation in 2017. Water, air, earth and waste materials are some natural elements currently being used to generate electric power. There are more discoveries coming. The United States EPA reported that "Hydropower plants produced about 7% of total U.S. electricity generation and about 44% of electricity generation from renewable energy in 2017". "Wind energy was the source of about 6% of total U.S. electricity generation and about 37% of electricity generation from renewable energy in 2017. "Biomass, the source of about 2% of total U.S. electricity generation in 2017". "Solar energy provided about 1% of total U.S. electricity in 2017". Nigeria's electricity generation problem will be resolved when we come to this understanding: there is electricity all around us, we only need to discover new ways to generate and distribute it.

INTERNET

Fiber optics is a tube, as thin as the human hair, quoted as a mirror. What is being sent is light travelling at record speed, which bounces on the wall of the tube. The limitation in the cable connection is the speed. Goes back to the problem of light in Nigeria. These bring into perspective the depths of the wisdom of God.

I was chatting with our pastor friend from California on the phone. I had never visited their Church, but we spoke on the phone whenever we could. He noticed that whenever there was a major event coming up at their Church, there would be an electricity outage. I began prayers right there on the phone. I heard God said, "there's deep witchcraft activities in that Church set to frustrate their efforts". God also said, "tell him I want to show him something on their corridor", I asked, "is there a corridor at your Church"? He said yes, that's where I am standing. Then I told him God said He wanted to show him something on the corridor. We continued to pray. About a week after, he said there was a door on the corridor that had never been opened since they leased the Church building. The landlord didn't have the keys nor did anyone have the keys in the Church. He said the landlord instructed them to break the door to see what was happening. They found switches connected to the building's power. And the switch went on and off at random. The question is: "Who was manipulating the switches as major Church events approached"? "What was the motive"?. Evil agents have understandings on how to ruin events. They knew if they kept the light out, nothing would work. That's the work of the enemy; they steal light so that they can perpetuate evil in darkness.

All the findings of science on light points back to the great works of God in the creation of the earth. How then can a nation who sheds innocent blood, loot national funds expect not to be a partaker of the "curse of darkness" as pronounced by God in Job 38:15a - The wicked are denied light?

This is the affliction battling Nigeria. Nigeria's many problems spurs from the romantic relationship between the country and darkness permissible through the weak spiritual state of the Church. Until the Church repents and prays for the baptism of the Holy Spirit will the electricity problem in Nigeria be resolved. Only then would Nigeria thrive economically again.

THE HOLY SPIRIT AS WISDOM

The Spirit of Wisdom sheds light on dark areas. It brings light to ignorance. It provides solutions to complex problems. The spirit of wisdom sheds light on dark regions. When the spirit of Wisdom shows up with a surprising fact.

Proverbs 8:22-31

> "The LORD brought me forth as the first of His works, before His deeds of old; I was formed long ages ago, at the very beginning, when the world came to be. When there were no watery depths, I was given birth, when there were no springs overflowing with water; before the mountains were settled in place, before the hills, I was given birth, before He made the world or its fields or any of the dust of the earth. I was there when He set the heavens in place, when He marked out the horizon on the face of the deep, when He established the clouds above and fixed securely the fountains of the deep, when He gave the sea its boundary so the waters would not overstep His command, and when He marked out the foundations of the earth. Then I was constantly at His side. I was filled with delight day after day, rejoicing always in his presence, rejoicing in his whole world and delighting in mankind.

Similar to artificial intelligence or machine learning where computers are trained to outperform humans in certain tasks using large pools of examples, data and experiences. God created wisdom before any other creation. Before the heavens were created, or the earth was formed, wisdom had existed. Wisdom is godly intelligence. Wisdom was present as the Lord created. God created the Spirit of wisdom to learn His processes. Any person whom the spirit of wisdom indwells has access to the intelligence of God for simplifying any form of complexity life may present. The Spirit of wisdom is another display of the power of the Holy Spirit.

THE HOLY SPIRIT AS FIRE

Fire doesn't joke. The test of fire is fierce. Purity is assured thereafter. The Holy Spirit is a purifier. Nigeria isn't a silver nation, it is a gold nation. A nation with tendencies of greatness. Nigeria is a nation God is deeply interested in displaying His glory upon. A giant nation covered in muds. A nation God is ready to thoroughly cleanse. He is going to cleanse with the firepower of the Holy Spirit. No one knows for sure how this will come into play, but the full display of Proverbs 17:3 is to be anticipated.

"The refining pot is for silver and the furnace for gold, But the LORD tests the hearts."

The melting point for silver is 961.8 degrees Celsius - 1763 degrees Fahrenheit. The melting for gold is 1064 degrees Celsius - 1948 Fahrenheit. To complete its refinement cycle, gold rises at a higher temperature than other less precious metals. It is during the melting process that impurities fall off and the genuineness of gold is proven. The varying temperatures indicate the different degrees of temperature needed for each metal type to come out in its purest form. The greater the depth of your test, the more likely that you are of higher value. The same with Nigeria, before the nation encounters the next great outpouring of the Holy Spirit, the

Church will be shaken and wickedness will be expunged from it. Nigeria is about to go through a similar refining cycle for revival to break loose, and influence to be restored to the Church.

THE HOLY SPIRIT AS WATER

The Scriptures described the Holy Spirit as water. Water brings forth cleanliness. It represents the cleansing power of the Holy Spirit. It also represents the source of life. Jesus spoke about the Holy Spirit.

John 7:37-39

> Now on the last day, the great day of the feast, Jesus stood and cried out, saying, "If anyone is thirsty, let him come to Me and drink. "He who believes in Me, as the Scripture said, 'From his innermost being will flow rivers of living water.'" But this He spoke of the Spirit, whom those who believed in Him were to receive; for the Spirit was not yet given, because Jesus was not yet glorified

Prophet Isaiah also spoke about the Holy Spirit in relation to water in

Isaiah 44:3.

> This verse is one of the Bible prophecies wrapped in parables. "For I will pour out water on the thirsty land And streams on the dry ground; I will pour out My

Spirit on your offspring And My blessing on your descendants".

A parable was used to bring one of the functions of the Holy Spirit to light. The word "Parable" is of Greek origin and it means "comparison.

Verse portion A: For I will pour out water on the thirsty land And streams on the dry ground. To pour means to "cause a liquid to flow from a container in a steady stream". To pour means to "send fluid or anything in loose particles from one container to another. (Dictionary.com). In Verse portion A: The Lord promises to pour out water on a thirsty land and streams on the dry ground. Agricultural sciences help us understand the value of water. A thirsty and dry land needs irrigation to thrive or to bring forth any fruit. Thirsty land means spiritual hunger. People who are hungry for the power of the Lord and His righteousness.

Verse portion B: I will pour out My Spirit on your offspring And My blessing on your descendants". Then verse portion B goes on to give us the meaning of the figurative expression. "Offspring" means the seed. Whenever a seed is planted, all conditions being equal, a growth is expected. Blessings talk about fruitfulness.

The Isaiah 44: 3 leads to one conclusion, fruitfulness and blessings come from the Holy Spirit upon the hearts of those who hunger for the Lord. The entire Isaiah 44 was the blessings of God being declared upon Israel as a nation. The prophecy does not end with Israel; it extends to any nation that hungers for the righteousness of the Lord.

Jeremiah 18:8

> Then the word of the Lord came to me, saying: "O house of Israel, can I not do with you as this potter?" says the Lord. "Look, as the clay *is* in the potter's hand, so *are* you in My hand, O house of Israel! The instant I speak concerning a nation and concerning a kingdom, to pluck up, to pull down, and to destroy *it*, if that nation against whom I have spoken turns from its evil, I will relent of the disaster that I thought to bring upon it. And the instant I speak concerning a nation and concerning a kingdom, to build and to plant *it*, if it does evil in My sight so that it does not obey My voice, then I will relent concerning the good with which I said I would benefit it.

The solution to Nigeria's eroding infrastructure such as electric power, quality education, healthcare , clean water and sanitation can be summed up in the person of the HOLY SPIRIT.

The Holy Spirit brings deep insights in the form of light from the mind of the Lord, to illuminate dark places of the earth. Dark places that are given to reprobate minds will not enjoy the benefits of the Holy Spirit.

Water, Wind, Light and the earth are all God's creations that scientists have generated electricity from. Financial bottlenecks and an unwilling government are not the major cause of lack of electricity, but the problem is a reflection of the spiritual state of the Church. That is what is really going on in the spiritual realm. When the few remnants rise up and lead the nations to the Acts exercise where people gather in groups of 4s and 5s all across and wait upon the Lord. The Holy Spirit will come down and God's people will burst into tongues. The fire of the Holy Spirit will be ignited, it will be sparked across the gatherings of the remnants and the Holy Spirit will sweep across the nation. The wind of God will blow away the chaff and the Holy Spirit will quicken the hearts of the Bezalel kind of scientist who will be shown the pattern of electricity distribution and supply from heaven.

As the wind of God blows, many sons and daughters will be commissioned to carry out the Great Commission. Sons and daughters who have grown deep in the Word of God and in the Power of the Holy Spirit. They will go into the harvest field all over Nigeria and begin to harvest for the kingdom. Signs and wonders will begin to follow. Many who have occupied seats and not bearing fruits will be uprooted.

A REPENTANT NATION

What would a repentant Church look like? When the Churches go back to God and say they have turned a new leaf or have a change of heart? Or when they say they are sorry? Only God knows, He alone will be able to search each heart and tell if the Church repents. One of the signs of genuine repentance would be the visibility of the fruits of righteousness. A repentant Nigeria will pursue righteousness. Good times will return, the Holy Spirit will move in our Churches, new innovation from Nigeria will be recorded, revivals will explode across cities, electricity problems will be resolved, the economy will see the light of the day and the Church will be seen as a sanctified organization.

Jeremiah 6:16a

> Stand in the ways and see,
> And ask for the old paths, where the good way is,
> Then you will find rest for your souls

FRUITFUL CHURCH, FRUITFUL NATION

Many have asked, when would Nigeria get better? Nigeria will only get better when the Church becomes fruitful. Budding is a culture of the Kingdom of God. It is a symbol of the Vine and the fruitful branch. One of the reasons Aaron's rod that budded was kept in the earthly tabernacle is to serve as a reminder of the fruitfulness that comes from the lives and nations that are chosen by the Lord.

Nigeria has not budded beyond her salvation times - when the Church came into Nigeria. There has been great decline in the recent decades across major industries, and the spiritual atmosphere is dark. Nigeria has many prophetic roles to fulfill. Nigeria will start to walk into these roles beginning 2020, and Nigeria will be catapulted into the world stage, taking the rest of Africa with her.

Before the time of fruitfulness comes, Nigeria has to be pruned. Nigeria currently harbors evil and is full of harlotry, serving Baal, worshipping the gods of fame, god of money, god of academic heights, and all other gods. When the time of pruning comes, everyone will run back to the

Lord. Jesus tells us in John 15:2 - "He cuts off every branch in me that bears no fruit, while every branch that does bear fruit he prunes so that it will even be more fruitful". An unfruitful branch does not need pruning. that explains the words of the Prophet in Jeremiah 8:20 - "The harvest is past, The summer is ended, And we are not saved". For as many as are left untamed, no fruitfulness is expected. Nigeria has a glorious destiny to birth, hence the Lord will prune, for the glorious delivery of a prophetic fruit. A fruitful nation will be spiritually blessed. The physical realm is a replay of the spiritual realm. If an environment is blessed spiritually, you experience success in the physical endeavors in that atmosphere. When the spiritual climate of Nigeria changes, the economy, academics, financial and all other sectors will thrive and a time of refreshing will come to the inhabitants of the nation. The Lord wants us to be fruitful, and He said, "this is to my Father's glory, that you bear much fruit, showing yourself to be my disciples" - John 15:7. As disciples of Jesus, It is the delight of our Father that we become fruitful. The Church in Nigeria must begin to produce fruits to the delight of the father. The Church must be connected deeper to the source of the Living Water to be fruitful. A life must be plugged into Jesus. A fruitful Church must remain in Jesus just as Aaron's rod was laid before the Lord. "And Moses placed the rods before the Lord in the tabernacle of witness. Now it came to pass on the next day that Moses went into the tabernacle of witness, and behold the rod of Aaron, of the house of Levi, had sprouted and put forth buds, had produced blossoms and yielded ripe almonds" Numbers 17:7-8.

Pruning is a constant part of Christian life. Pruning is God resizing and reshaping us to fit into His image, which He made us to be originally. The pruning process takes away the filths and toxins that stand in our way of growth beyond salvation. As a Gardner takes away the weed from the plants, so will the Lord take away impurities from our dear Nigeria to reshape Nigeria for His purpose.

Christianity will be restored to its Jewish roots, where we will experience apostolic movements, greater than historic revival movements.

GOD'S JUDGEMENT

Many have been led astray because of the ways of certain ministers of God. If the Church and these leaders will not turn back, God's judgment is coming against them in 2019, through the results of the election. The majority of the ministers from Nigeria we see on social media are building a following to disciple them on how to lust after earthly wealth, by showcasing their amassed possessions and luxury experience - confusing unbelievers to stray further from the Way, and painting the wrong picture of Christianity. Only the remnants engage their followers with the scriptures.

As the Lord is set to prune the Church in Nigeria, we do not know how He intends to, but it will have an overall picture of removing the weeds from the plants. Jeremiah 1:10 will also be resurfaced. Churches and ministers that have been planted in the wrong foundation will be taken through a season of digging and uprooting from the faulty foundations. The ones who repent early enough will be replanted and rebuilt. The Lord will be merciful to those who are contrite in heart. For those who have made a mockery of God's calling, they will reap judgment, for the cup of many is full. Those who have gone off God's course need to rectify their way to make their ways right as soon as possible.

Romans 11:17

> "For if the first fruit is holy, the lump is also holy; and if the root is holy, so are the branches. And if some of the branches were broken off, and you, being a wild olive tree, were grafted in among them, and with them became a partaker of the root and fatness of the olive tree"

Those who use the altar as a place of intimidation will be made of no irrelevance by the Lord. Many who fleece the sheep will be exposed and some will go into hiding. The remnants ministers of the Lord shall stand and decree uncompromisingly the word of God over the nations. Through the remnants, the name of the Lord, the raw power of YHWH, and His undiluted love will be made known to the masses.

12

THE UPCOMING REVIVAL

THE COMING CHANGE

The nation is going to undergo such a rapid change if the Church turns back that people will be begging to return to Nigeria. There is going to be great technological and spiritual advancement. The people shall locate their source again. They will locate the Lord. The next move of God's power is going to come through Africa. Africa will come into power. The continent of Africa will be used to take center place in Africa again. The Lord is building up leaders who have gone into captivity, and applied their hearts to wisdom. He is taking them back to Africa to build, uncompromisingly righteous leaders, who will go back to fight against the enemy and iniquity.

Your prayers and intercession is needed for Nigeria. Believers, rise up in prayers to avert this situation. As you commute, back and forth to work, or carry out your daily routine, pray for Nigeria.

The word of God needs to permeate into every sphere of the society. It has to be where everyone will return back to the Scripture to individually discover the Ancient God of the Scriptures and not what the society has painted God to be.

The Lord will raise godly leaders that will move in the power of the Holy Spirit to set things right across the nation. A time is coming when only the name of the Lord will be instilled in the laws of the land. A movement for small groups of Bible Studies, holiness, humility will begin, which will take Nigeria from where it is right now to where it needs to be.

All these good news starts with you and I. Here's your part in it.

WHAT YOU CAN DO FOR NIGERIA

Personal Growth Plan

Everyone needs to look inwardly and repent for departing from the ways of the Lord. Starting from the youth who have been rude to the elders and to those who sin or a minor scale and condemn the people in government who are running Nigeria dry. The leaders in government need to repent too. Nigerians at home and in diaspora need to repent. We all need to repent. We also need to become better - for some, it will be learning to stay humble, for some integrity and for others, it will be learning to stay away from all forms of hate.

Create a Worship and Prayer Network of Five

Your primary manner of engagement is to go on your knees for Nigeria. It will not help to criticize others. Pray to God for the change you want to see. Invite your friends to intercede for Nigeria as well. To encourage you, build a network of 5 friends to pray together for Nigeria. Encourage other 5 friends to start their prayer network too.

Group Bible Study

People need to boldly take the word of God into the communities. No longer should Scriptural studies be confined to the Church or made a Sunday school affair. Be encouraged to form a small Bible study group to meet at lunch time or weekends. Students and young adults, older workers and retirees - we all need to get grounded, stir up one another and connect directly to the word of God. This brings stability and prevents us from being led astray by demonic teachings of false teachers and prophets of Baal.

THESE ARE GREAT PRAYERS TO START WITH...

1. Lord Jesus, disgrace and nullify the counsel of the wicked over Nigeria and the continent of Africa.
2. Establish your government over the nation of Nigeria and the rest of Africa.
3. Father, Remove the altar of desecration from Nigeria
4. Lord, uproot the altar of darkness from Nigeria remove filth of the uncircumcised heart.
5. Cleanse your Church with the firepower of the Holy Spirit.
6. Nigeria will not return into slavery in the name of Jesus.
7. Lord, break the stronghold and demonic throne in Benin sitting on top of Nigeria.
8. Lord Jesus, uproot the stronghold of wickedness located in each city in Nigeria.
9. Thou yokes and demonic covenants of Calabar, holding Nigeria back, be broken in the name of Jesus.
10. Let the fire from the presence of the Lord strengthen the bars of the gates of Nigeria in the name of Jesus.
11. Thou demonic woman seated upon the throne, riding Nigeria as a caravan, let the judgment of God arise and unseat you in the name of Jesus.
12. Thou satanic woman who placed demonic carts and heavy yokes upon the back of the Nigerian people; let

the fire from the mouth of Yahweh devour you in the name of Jesus.

13. On behalf of Nigeria, Lord, break the yoke of love affair with demonic oppression in the name of Jesus.

14. Lord, break the yoke of promiscuity over Nigeria.

15. Let the spirit of legalism depart from our Churches.

16. Let the power and love of Jesus flow into the Churches.

17. Let the spirit of compromise depart from Church

18. Lord Jesus, place the seal of your name over Nigeria.

19. Lord let the altars of YHWH be revived in the name of Jesus.

20. Pray that the Lord grants you revelation on how to pray for Nigeria.

BIBLIOGRAPHY

HTTPS://WWW.PULSE.NG/COMMUNITIES/RELIGION/HERES-A-BRIEF-HISTORY-O
N-THE-FIRST-CHURCH-IN-NIGERIA-ID7574887.HTMLHTTP://WWW.PEWFORU
M.ORG/2006/10/05/HISTORICAL-OVERVIEW-OF-PENTECOSTALISM-IN-NIGERIA
/

HTTPS://WWW.EIA.GOV/ENERGYEXPLAINED/INDEX.PHP?PAGE=ELECTRICITY_IN
_THE_UNITED_STATES (ENGERGY GENERATED IN THE US)

HTTPS://LIBRARY.SI.EDU/EXHIBITION/COLOR-IN-A-NEW-LIGHT/SCIENCE

HTTP://GALILEOANDEINSTEIN.PHYSICS.VIRGINIA.EDU/LECTURES/SPEDLITE.HTM
L (SEEPD OF LIGHT)

HTTPS://WWW.FI.EDU/BENJAMIN-FRANKLIN/KITE-KEY-EXPERIMENT

HTTPS://WEB.ARCHIVE.ORG/WEB/20150409000235/HTTP://HOMECOMINGREV
OLUTION.COM/NIGERIA/2014/05/13/NEW-YORK-LAGOS-INSPIRATION-BEHIND-
NEW-TAXI-APP-NIGERIA/

HTTPS://PDXSCHOLAR.LIBRARY.PDX.EDU/CGI/VIEWCONTENT.CGI?REFERER=HTT
PS://WWW.GOOGLE.COM/&HTTPSREDIR=1&ARTICLE=1955&CONTEXT=OPEN_A
CCESS_ETDS

HTTPS://WWW.NBCNEWS.COM/FEATURE/NBC-OUT/OBAMA-LEGACY-QUIET-MISS
ION-EXPORT-GAY-RIGHTS-OVERSEAS-N673861

HTTP://WWW.AKA-IKENGA.COM/2012/10/THE-ROLE-OF-CHURCH-IN-BIAFRA.
HTML

OTHER BOOKS BY EBENEZER & ABIGAIL GABRIELS

A Prophetic Call to Revive Dead Altars

AMERICA
The Past, Present & The
NEXT CHAPTER

Ebenezer Gabriels
Abigail Gabriels

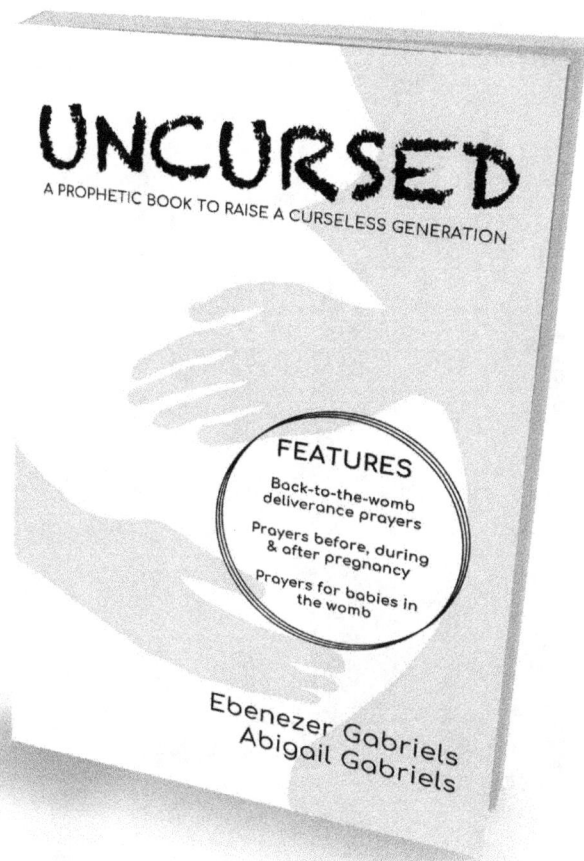

UNCURSED - A PROPHETIC BOOK TO RAISE A CURSELESS GENERATION

Back-to-the womb deliverance is rarely conducted by most Christians. Jabez prayed this manner of prayer, David's actions led into curses that affected his household. Everyone, babies in the womb, babies already born, adult children, adults all need to be delivered from lingering curses regardless of how long they have been in the Christian faith.

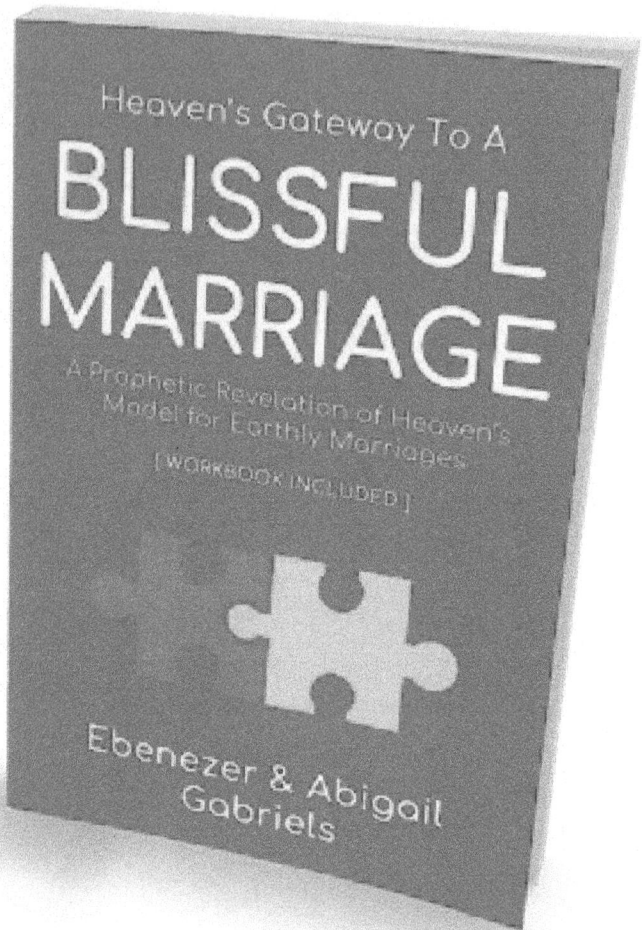

HEAVEN'S GATEWAY TO A BLISSFUL MARRIAGE

How do you rebuild your marriage and make it what God meant for it to be? How do you engage in spiritual warfare for your marriage? How do you cultivate the culture of heaven in your marriage? Heaven's gateway to a Blissful Marriage shows every couple the model of God for a blessed, sanctified, renewed, whole and blissful marriage. This book walks couples through God's design and intent for marriages.

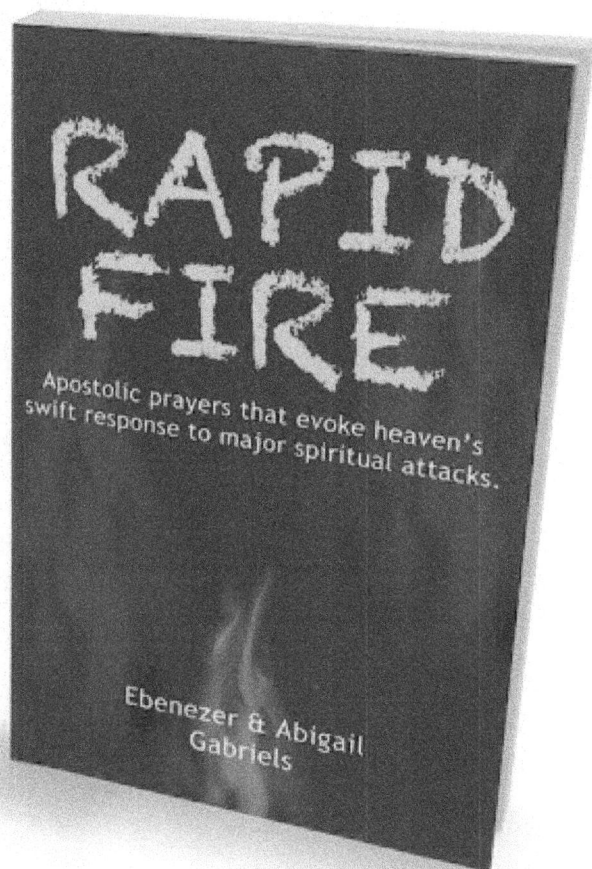

RAPID FIRE
Learn the principles of intense spiritual warfare like the Apostles'. The kind o f prayers that delivered David from the hands of His enemies. 10 common areas of attacks are covered: Spiritual growth, marriage, untimely death, health, witchcraft attacks, mind and brain attacks, finances and foundation. Rapid Fire is a manual that teaches believers how to disrupt satanic harassment and oppression through radical prayers.

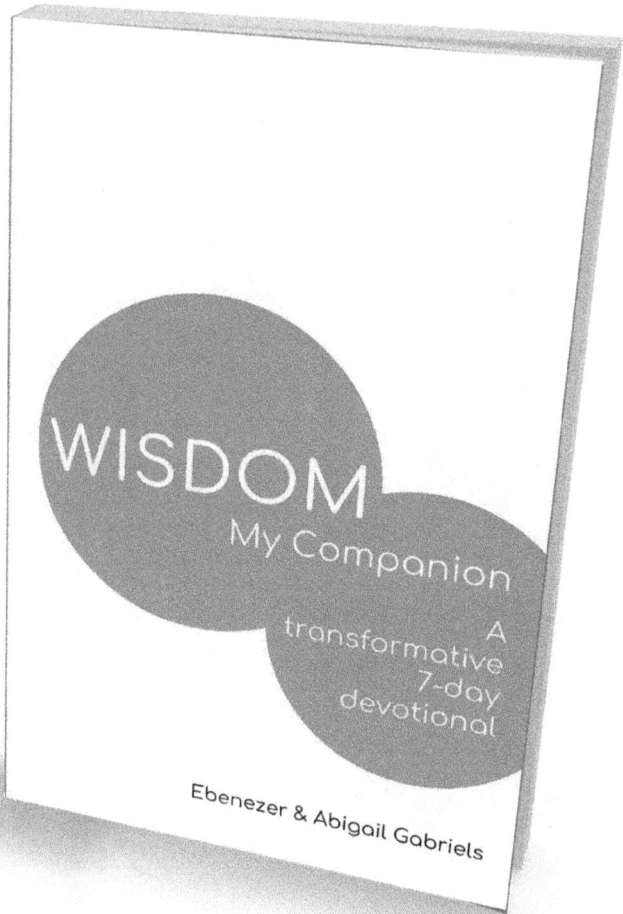

WISDOM MY COMPANION

Wisdom is a 7-day devotional to help you learn about heavenly wisdom and how to integrate Kingdom's wisdom into everyday experience. This book teaches how to deal with practical affairs of everyday life from Heaven's perspective and touches on subjects like parenting, leadership, money management, and home-building,

ABOUT THE AUTHORS

Ebenezer is Worshipper, Prophet and Intercessor. He worships on the Piano. He is called in the marketplace as a Technologist. In the marketplace, he is a Software Architect and Machine Learning Consultant building algorithms and platforms that bring Heaven's glory into organizations around the world.

Abigail is a Worshipper, Pastor, Intercessor and Writer. Abigail worships on the Saxophone and blows the Shofar. In the marketplace, she is a Data Scientist with a focus on Predictive Analytics, Natural Language Processing and Sentiment Mining, helping the world makes sense out of data.

Ebenezer and Abigail pastors LightHill Church in Maryland and are the founders of the Ebenezer Gabriels Ministries. Their mandate is to revive worship altars and intercede for nations. Ebenezer is married to Abigail, and their lives are a testimony of the resurrection power of the Lord.

EGƎ

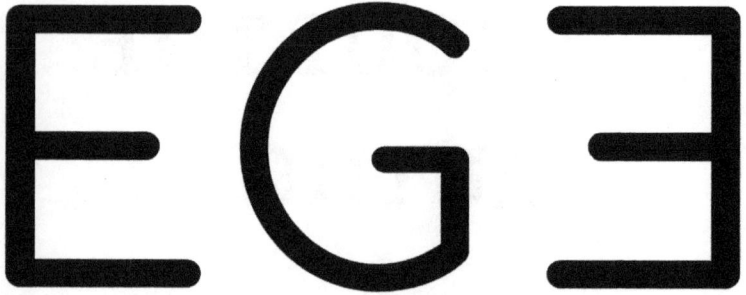

Ebenezer Gabriels Ministries

EGM provides resources for people to encounter Jesus. Our mandate is deep worship and to share the unfiltered word of God. The ministry is eager to see people delivered from captivity, and for wayward sons and daughters to return to the LORD.

EGM's arm of publishing designs and develops Christian resources inspired by the Lord. EGM currently operates out of Gaithersburg in Maryland, USA.

CONTACT US

hello@ebenezergabriels.org | www.ebenezergabriels.org

Other Books By Ebenzer & Abigail Gabriels

www.ingramcontent.com/pod-product-compliance
Lightning Source LLC
LaVergne TN
LVHW011332080426
835513LV00006B/308